May Abba's personal love
for you be revealed through
these meditations

Alyce Lo Bianco

MEDITATIONS

FROM YOUR

FATHER

Daily Messages From God

ALYSE LO BIANCO

All Scripture quotations are taken from the
HOLY BIBLE, NEW INTERNATIONAL VERSION (NIV)
Copyright 1973,1978, 1984, 2011
by the International Bible Society

Cover and book design by The Book Cover Whisperer:
ProfessionalBookCoverDesign.com

Printed in the United States of America.

ISBN: 978-1-7341370-2-6 Hardcover
ISBN: 978-1-7341370-0-2 Paperback
ISBN: 978-1-7341370-1-9 eBook

SECOND EDITION

Foreword

THE FOLLOWING MESSAGES of love and encouragement were given to me when I was undergoing an extremely difficult time in my life. My husband and stepfather had died a day apart from each other two years before, and I was under incredible financial pressure and depression because of it. My fears were so great that each morning when I woke up, I longed to be someone else!

When I first arose each morning, I would go to my quiet place, start with praise and worship, read the Bible and then journal my pleas for help and guidance to the Lord. His presence would settle over me gently, and I was filled with peace. I started writing down what He impressed upon me. Sometimes it was a slow, word-by-word guidance, and at other times, whole sentences would tumble out faster than I could write them down. He shared such words of love!

I was born in a home for unwed mothers and did not go to live with my mother until I was ten years old. It was only when I became an adult that she learned to hug me, and because of that, my greatest unmet desire as a child was to be touched and held. At night I would kneel at my bedroom window and beg God to come down and hold me.

At the age of 15, a young man shared John 3:16 with me at the base of a mountain in Yosemite, and my world changed. Those words pierced my soul with joy. I was really loved!! But because of my upbringing, my insecurities were great.

I was definitely not a planned child, therefore, how could the promises in the Bible be true for me? Yet when God started revealing His messages to me years later, He told me that He Himself had planned my existence before the beginning of the world, and that He would always guide and take care of me, and that yes, those Bible promises were true for me, and for every believer.

I sense that God Himself sent me these love letters because He knew that my greatest need was for a father. Yet sometimes it was clear that Jesus was also speaking through with His words of love.

I started sharing a few of these love letters with my friends, and they then passed them along to their friends. Over and over people would email me to say that a particular letter must have been written just for them: *How did God know what was going on in their house that exact day? How did He know their inner fears?*

I struggled with the fact that even though the messages are all a little different, they have much the same message. Every morning as I waited quietly for the words, I prayed that He would share something different than before. But the Lord deeply impressed me with several things:

1. At the beginning of every day, and in fact, all throughout the day, He wants us to focus on Him.
2. Our focus should be on how much He loves us, how close He is to us, and how He longs for us to ask for His help and for His constant presence in our lives.

These are the deepest needs of those He has chosen to reveal Himself to.

These letters offer a good base for discussions of God's love. Many people have told me that they have recommitted their lives to Christ after reading these, found great comfort during their losses and struggles and learned how real, how strong and how personal the Lord's love is for them.

What I have discovered from these messages, and from the response of others who have read them, is that our God is the most AWESOME, LOVING Heavenly Father. He is our Daddy, our Healer, our Holder and Hugger. His sacrifices for us were immense.

When I read these words from Him even today, a peace sweeps over me as the fear in my heart leaves.

Thank You, Lord. You alone are Holy. You alone are Good.

Please come with open hearts every day and learn to envision His real presence and love for you. It cries to the soul of every one of us, and it is real. He is real, and He wants you to know He is right beside you always, loving you in ways you could never be loved by anyone on earth.

Brothers and sisters, may you be blessed as you read these letters written by your Father to you.

Acknowledgement

I WOULD LIKE TO thank the Lord for His beautiful words of love in this book. And for the wonderful family that He has so richly blessed me with: my husband, Tony, my daughter, Lanah Fitzgerald and her husband Tom; my son, Tristan Hamilton, and his wife, April, and my wonderful grandchildren, Tennyson, Milan, August and Geneva. Each of you is a gift and have captured my heart completely.

January 01

I am near to you now. So close. So real. Close your eyes and sense My presence.

All your life you have longed for a love that is true and pure. You are starting to sense it as you draw closer to Me through our time together.

Thank you for seeking Me, dear one. For seeking not only to know Me, but to draw into My presence.

Our communion together is very precious to Me. You will never regret this time we spend together.

Use our encounter throughout the day. Call out My name when you think you can't get through something. When challenges seem overwhelming, tap back into your memory of our time together.

Such peace I will give you, enabling you to soar like an eagle over the highest mountains.

You have an attachment to the Almighty that enables you to look down during your flight on all the cares of this world.

I make that possible, beloved one. Only through Me will you find peace through life's hardships.

Hold on now as we soar through the skies!

Even youths grow tired and weary, and young men stumble and fall; but those who hope in the Lord will renew their strength. They will soar on wings like eagles; they will run and not grow weary, they will walk and not be faint.
Isaiah 40:30-31

January 02

Do not fear that you are entering the lion's den, for no matter where you go, I will be beside you.

When the time comes for you to speak, do not fear what you will say, for I will put the right words in your mouth.

You are My child and I have chosen you to do this work.

There is so much you don't understand, yet I have planned this very day for you from the beginning of the world. It is not a fearful time, but a time for you to sit back and see how I work.

Let My glory unfold around you. People will know that you serve Me by how things are accomplished.

I am with you, dear one. That is all you need to know.

The King of the universe is with you. The Ruler of all stands beside you.

What have you to fear?

I have put My words in your mouth and covered you with the shadow of My hand - I who set the heavens in place, who laid the foundations of the earth, and Who say to Zion, "You are My people."
Isaiah 51:16

January 03

I have not made life easy for you.

If I love you so much, why haven't I? Isn't love about making life happy for those you care about?

Happiness is not about avoiding pain. It is in the joy and peace that I have given your soul when you trust Me through anything and everything.

Sometimes, things are so painful you don't think you can bear them any longer. That is when I need you to hang on tightly to Me, because I am even closer than before.

When you falter, I will be there to pick you up.

One day I will be able to pick you up in My arms and carry you to the place I have prepared for you. There you will know only pure joy.

No more sadness or pain. Total unadulterated joy.

Let Me bear your pain, beloved one, because I feel it deeper than you. You are not alone in this. Let Me wipe your tears on My shoulder.

Count on the joy to get you through. One day you will know it openly.

It was always there.

May the God of hope fill you with all joy and peace as you
trust in Him, so that you may overflow with hope
by the power of the Holy Spirit.
Romans 15:13

January 04

I am going to show you, dear one, the right way to go and the right thing to do. Just trust the still, small voice in your mind and soul. It is Me guiding you.

You will not wonder whether the voice is from is Me, you will know.

I have put you right here and now, to learn this trust. To practice trusting in Me will increase your knowledge, resulting in a stronger faith: a faith that will withstand the toughest challenges you will ever face in the future. Don't be frightened by that statement.

I have given you everything you need to face these challenges. You are armed mightily with your faith, and because of it, with Me at your side. Watch and see how I will work!

New stories are being written every day about how I have worked mightily here on earth! Our story is one of them.

The story of you and Me, and Me and you.

If not read here on earth, it will be recounted in Heaven with great joy at the outcome of the victory.

Hang on, dear child.
The greatest story of your life is yet to unfold.

Even in darkness light dawns for the upright, for those who are gracious and compassionate and righteous. They will have no fear of bad news; their hearts are steadfast, trusting in the Lord.
Psalm 112:4, 7

January 05

*D*o you think that I could ever forget you, My child? That your problems are not in the forefront of My mind?

I know they are there. These problems are right where I want them to be, right where you will grow to love and trust Me through your dealing with them. They are right where you will reach out to Me and ask Me to help you through your pain.

Dear one, I will hold you up and through it all.
I am your Lifeline.

I know the person you will become through all this.

You can't see it now, but you will mature into a strong leader, a leader who people going through the same situation will come to for encouragement and advice.

So, be encouraged and strong, dear one. There is light at the end of this tunnel and together we will walk through it.

What is mankind that you are mindful of them, a son of man
that you care for him? You made them a little lower than
the angels; You crowned them with glory and honor
and put everything under their feet.
Hebrews 2:6-8

January 06

*I*s your spirit troubled? Is the pain so intense you want to run and find something or someone to fill the void? You can't, dear one. The pain you are feeling needs to be felt and it needs to be dealt with.

You have experienced a loss and you must not run from its growth. There is a maturity that will come from all this, and a deeper relationship with Me. Only you and I together can see you through to the other side.

There are no quick fixes. Don't put someone in your life who stands to get hurt while you move through this journey. This is between you and Me.

Let Me hold you up every step, helping you through the large and small decisions of your life. One day you will be glad you took this time to renew your soul. It will prepare you for the new love I am sending to you when the time is right.

You cannot experience true joy with another until you have totally grieved your loss. Someday, this time with you and Me will be something you will look back at and cherish, even though you have found happiness again.

So come to Me, dear one. Only I can understand your pain. Only I know.

Come and rest your head on My shoulder. I will be your Rock.

The Lord is my rock, my fortress and my deliverer;
my God is my rock, in Whom I take refuge, my shield
and the horn of my salvation. He is my
stronghold, my refuge and my Savior
2 Samuel 22:2-3

January 07

*Y*ou are in a situation that has hurt you, but I will be your Rock. Lean your head on My shoulder and let Me comfort you.

Together we can face anything.

Remember the greater goal of bringing My lost sheep into the fold. Everything happens for a purpose. Your anger and subsequent hurt can be used as ammunition to gather yourself up in strength to face the giants in your life.

Girded with My full armor you can even reach out to those who have inflicted pain upon you. The door to evil and sin all starts with people experiencing pain in their own lives.

How will you react from the pain in yours? Let it strengthen you to become the mighty warrior I need you to be: the mighty warrior who finds their strength upon My shoulder.

Ever My child, growing into a mighty warrior for truth, justice and mercy.

Praise be to the God and Father of our Lord Jesus Christ, the Father of compassion and the God of all comfort, Who comforts us in all our troubles, so that we can comfort those in any trouble with the comfort we ourselves receive from God. For just as we share abundantly in the sufferings of Christ, so also our comfort abounds through Christ.
2 Corinthians 1:3-5

January 08

Let your joy rise up this morning, dear child. Joy that your soul is clean and free from sin and darkness; joy in the Lover of your soul.

Yes, you may still feel pain, but the joy of My presence rises up to overflowing. The peace that passes all understanding pours through your soul.

Oh, dear one, the rewards of making your camp with Me are great.

I may give you many earthly treasures, or you may be struggling for your most basic needs. I know exactly where you are, and what you are going through, and I will never let you down. I will never let you go.

As a child plays carefree in the rain, I am asking you to lay your burden at My feet and let Me bear it.

Come and let Me wrap My arms around you in an everlasting circle of love. Let the joy bubble up, over and under you.

Look up, dear one, and smile, for your Joy is here.

Your Joy is near.

You have loved righteousness and hated wickedness;
therefore God, your God, has set you above your
companions by anointing you with the oil of joy.
Hebrews 1:9

January 09

*D*id you awaken this morning saying, "I choose You!"?

Let those words be your first conscious thoughts and dedication of the day. In so doing, all Heaven's power will be at your disposal against the evil one.

Those three simple words knock the devil right off his pedestal, and away from being able to infiltrate your life for that moment.

"I choose You!" is like saying "I choose life and power through Jesus Christ."

Say "I Choose You!" through the most difficult of situations. Say "I choose You!" through pain, sorrow and disappointment.

What a gift to My ears! You will be rewarded, dear one. I will draw you closer into My presence. It is your words of love and commitment that are so special to Me.

Put those three powerful words into practice today.

Those who know Your name trust in You, for You, Lord,
have never forsaken those who seek You.
Psalm 9:10

January 10

Come to Me this morning with the burdens of your day. Lay them at My feet and I will cover you with a blanket of peace.

My peace is something more extravagant than what you find here on earth. It is all-encompassing; a total feeling that washes over you from the top of your head to the end of each toe. My peace is like softly rocking waves on a lake, gently lapping at the sides of a boat.

But how do you experience this peace? By recognizing Me as your Savior and accepting the gift of life because My Son died for you.

Seems pretty easy, doesn't it? Yet, to many, it is not. They reject this ultimate Gift and harden their hearts towards Me.

Do not let satan harden your heart.

Accept My gift, and the peace that passes all understanding will flood the gates of your soul as My presence enters in.

Daily lay your burdens at My feet so that your joy may be complete.

Do not be anxious about anything, but in every situation, by prayer and petition, with thanksgiving, present your requests to God. And the peace of God, which transcends all understanding, will guard your hearts and your minds in Christ Jesus.
Philippians 4:6-7

January 11

Have I not already accepted you as one of My own? Why do I ask you to renew your commitment to Me daily? To say, "I choose You!", over and over?

Beloved one, I chose you before the foundation of the world. I knew you and I loved you, yet there is an evil presence lurking about, looking to devour My own.

When you start the day by committing it to Me, I am able to surround you with a wall of protection. satan is kept at bay.

Repeat the words throughout the day when you feel weak, tempted or scared. Call out My name. You will immediately be surrounded by a heavenly host much more powerful than the evil one lurking about, desperately trying to get My chosen ones to falter. He knows he only has a short time left and he is trying as hard as he can.

Rest safely in the security of My love and care for you. Read over the promises in the Bible.

You never need fear, dear one, when you open the day saying, "I choose You!", or just by calling out My Name.

You are safely in My fold, dear one. Now and forevermore.

And this is my prayer: that your love may abound more and more in knowledge and depth of insight, so that you may be able to discern what is best and may be pure and blameless for the day of Christ.
Philippians 1:9-10

January 12

Lasso your thoughts, dear one. Bring them in. Do not wander over past evil and pain in your life. Yes, you have sinned, and others have sinned against you, but do not let these thoughts permeate your being.

You have been saved, cleansed, and washed by the blood of Jesus. He alone was able to give you this gift by His terrible sacrifice on the cross.

Embrace it in every way. Move forward, not backwards. Your past life is not just years that mark your age, it is your testimony to help others.

It is the story of how Christ has triumphed in you, bringing you to joy and salvation!!

Let love overflow from your veins as you minister to others who have caused you past pain. It is over and done because you have left the pain at the cross and your life is fresh and new in Me every day.

Only those who walk with Me will understand. They, like you, have experienced love that knows no regret or past scars, only the pure testimony of lives transformed.

Share this love, dear one. It is your joy . . . and Mine.

And you also were included in Christ when you heard the
message of truth, the gospel of your salvation. When you
believed, you were marked in Him with a seal, the promised
Holy Spirit Who is a deposit guaranteeing our inheritance
until the redemption of those who are God's possession -
to the praise of His glory.
Ephesians 1:13-14

January 13

How a light shines on a hill when the night is clear! That is how your light should shine to others in need.

Who are those in need? Those closest to you. God has put the people around you in your path for your own personal ministry.

You don't have to be a pastor to have a ministry. I have put you right where you are for a reason. Don't wait until I put you in front of a large group to save others. Start right where you are!

Reach out with a phone call, a hug, or a small gift you made or purchased, just to let them know they are loved and thought about.

The world's greatest need is to be loved.

I have shown you My love so that you may share it with others. You are My light on a hill. Come and let Me permeate your soul anew so that you may have a clearer understanding of the mission.

Yes, I will use you for great things, but great things start right in front of you, right around you.

Reach out now. I will be beside you and will guide and direct you.

Share My love, beloved one. Share My love.

Instead, speaking the truth in love, we will grow to become
in every respect the mature body of Him who
is the head, that is, Christ.
Ephesians 4:15

January 14

By now you are aware of My movement in your life, movement in small waves. But I am ready to start moving more heavily in your life.

A true commitment to Me, total surrender, enables you to move into a union with Me very few Christians have experienced.

Come and see the joy of walking with Me. Everything you do now will be considered by the light of the knowledge of My presence.

Things will seem clearer, you will sense doors opening or closing, and you will be more aware of My gentle urges towards something, or away from it.

Surrender fully, dear one.

Let Me guide you to the life of freedom I have planned for you. One where you will walk openly with Me.

> *"My sheep listen to My voice; I know them, and they follow Me. I give them eternal life, and they shall never perish; no one will snatch them out of My hand. My Father, who has given them to Me, is greater than all; no one can snatch them out of My Father's hand. I and the Father are One."*
> *John 10:27-30*

January 15

I am here beside you now. Sometimes you doubt that, but My presence is as real as the fingers on your hand.

Close your eyes and think of Me. Envision Me as I walked with the disciples. Earthly pictures may come into your mind, pictures artists have penned throughout the years, or I may give you a clearer vision. The image in your mind is not what matters. It is the comfort you draw from being able to envision My nearness in a real way.

If you saw Me in My full glory, you would not be able to look or even to stand.

What I want you to take away from this is the reality of a loving Savior tenderly watching over you. Keep the image real, and when you call My name, imagine being able to look at Me.

One day you will be able to, beloved one. Right now, I will only give you glimpses in your mind to hang on to. But soon we will be together.

Until then, close your eyes and know, really know, I am beside you now.

You are never alone.

He tends His flock like a shepherd: He gathers the lambs in His arms and carries them close to His heart; He gently leads those that have young.
Isaiah 40:11

January 16

Was I disappointed in you when you were thinking about your own accomplishments and your own worth?

I am saddened when I see your rejection of the simple life I offer you and when I watch you grasping for the things of this earth: the glitz, the noise, the attention. Yet, I put you there to see how you would react.

Are you ready to be part of the world again?
Or, do you feel a need to spend time with Me?

I have put you here for a reason. As My child, you are My emissary to bring My light and love to others. Are you ready to be back in the world or do you need to come apart awhile longer, steeping yourself in My love?

I need you, dear one. You are one of My chosen soldiers. Take whatever time you need to be fully charged again with the ammunition of love and light. Then, when you are ready, don My armor.

I will be with you wherever you go.
We have a work to do, beloved one.

Don't let go of My hand.

> *But since we belong to the day, let us be sober, putting on faith and love as a breastplate, and the hope of salvation as a helmet. For God did not appoint us to suffer wrath but to receive salvation through our Lord Jesus Christ.*
> *I Thessalonians 5:8-9*

January 17

𝒟o you wish to say eloquent words, My love? I don't need eloquent. I need only words of love and hope to a dying world.

The world is hard and cynical. Things are happening quickly. Stay close to Me and spread My love to a generation of people aching inside. So many of them are full of pain from the hurts that are escalating all around as evil and the maker of it abounds.

There is one message of the gospel: Christ and Him crucified. One Savior and one message.

I have been preparing you to share it with others. Nothing else matters.

Christ in that message is love so acute the world cannot hold it.

There are many different religions, theologies and world views, but only one way to Me: Christ and Him crucified. That is your message.

Let the theologians of the world pick apart the intricacies of the gospel. They make it complicated, and yet it is so simple because it all boils down to love. Love so intense and so personal, and so real between you and Me.

Let others know, dear one. Let them know.

And so it was with me, brothers and sisters. When I came to you, I did not come with eloquence or human wisdom as I proclaimed to you the testimony about God. For I resolved to know nothing while I was with you except Jesus Christ and Him crucified.
I Corinthians 2:1-2

January 18

Thank you for rising up to come to Me.

Breathe Me in deeply into your soul. You are in My favor, dear one. I will answer your heartfelt desires and prayers.

How I love watching you! I watch your every move. From the time you arise to stretch on the side of the bed; as you walk sleepily into the bathroom and start the day, My eyes are on you.

Did you rise early enough to spend time with Me? Did you dedicate your life to Me the first thing?

Do you ever think of My needs, the all-powerful God Who always loves and takes care of you? It is such joy to Me when you seek Me, when you tell Me of your love for Me, when you express your devotion to Me by reaching out to others. I created you to love and serve Me. I am a jealous God who wants and needs His children close beside Him.

Yes, there are many people who feel good when they can help others. There are many people who work long and hard to improve the lives of others without knowing the Reason behind their drive other than that they "feel good."

But you and I have a bond that ties us to each other now and throughout all eternity. Just take one step at a time. I will lead you there.

I will remain in the world no longer, but they are still in the world, and I am coming to You. Holy Father, protect them by the power of Your name, the name You gave Me, so that they may be one as We are one.
John 17:11

January 19

Let Me fill you up today with the fullness of My love. Let it overflow from your pores, spreading out to those around you.

Close your eyes and feel My presence.

I am your daddy, yet I am your God. Do not disobey what I have commanded you to do.

As the winter winds flow around you in a fierce manner, like a firm young tree you will stand strong and tall.

My Word will protect you.
My words will shield you.

Study and know the verses and be able to bring them to mind when you are troubled, for these promises from Me will calm the fierce winds and you will safely nestle in My love and care.

Oh, dear one, stay connected.

Choose Me,
for I have chosen you.

"Because he loves me," says the Lord, "I will rescue him;
I will protect him, for he acknowledges My name."
Psalm 91:14

January 20

You are crying out to Me from the depths of your soul.

Others see you as secure and happy. I know your soul and it cries to Me of pain and fear.

Dear one, don't you know I have conquered all? Don't you know I have you in the palm of My hand? I know what you are going through. I have been there with you every step of the way.

Do not fear.
I will help you through this.

In the Bible, Samuel took a stone and set it between Mizpah and Shen and named the stone Ebenezer. He said "Thus far the Lord has helped us."

Find your own "thus far" rock and keep it in a place where you can look at it or come to it often to remember how I have led you safely "thus far" through seemingly impossible waters, and that I will continue to lead you until you are safely in My arms.

"Thus far", beloved, and thus forever in My love, My grace and My care.

Then Samuel took a stone and set it up between Mizpah
and Shen. He named it Ebenezer, saying,
"Thus far the Lord has helped us."
I Samuel 7:12

January 21

*D*o not be scared, My dear one. I am beside you.

The walls seem to be rising up around you but that is only because you have built them up in your mind.

I don't see walls. I see character-forming situations around you: situations I am waiting for you to draw closer to Me from.

Use this time and these problems to take steps towards Me, letting Me gather you into My arms. Learn to face them with total surrender to My will. Yes, with the passion that I have given you to conquer them, as well. A pure passion formed by total surrender to My will.

Do not sigh with the heaviness of the situation.
I have it in My hands.

Nothing is ever as bad as you imagine it to be because I am with you. I want you to grow to that level of trust.

Lose the binders that keep your vision on the problems. See everything around you that I have blessed you with.

There is SO MUCH, beloved, so very, very much.

"Thus Far" you have come.
"Thus far" I will carry you through.

> *Not only so, but we also glory in our sufferings, because we know that suffering produces perseverance; perseverance, character; and character, hope.*
> *Romans 5:3-4*

January 22

Be ever watchful today, dear one. Stay connected to Me as you go about your day. There are those who would have you fall, who work against Me by working against you.

Stay connected.
You have My power at your disposal.

Do not go through life seeming to be a helpless child. I have blessed you with strength and power you have not even tapped into yet. When you face your foes or your difficulties, if you but ask, you can arm yourself with My full coat of armor, protecting you from anything that is cast in your direction.

As My child, you have the ability to be a valiant soldier. But when you come to Me, there are no pretenses. Fold yourself into My loving arms, the more helpless the better, and I will hold you snug and secure.

These are our special times together where you gather that strength to face the world. Come to Me now, before the day gets away from you and let Me don your mighty armor.

To the world you are a strong warrior.
To Me, you are My beloved and precious child.

Therefore put on the full armor of God, so that when the day
of evil comes, you may be able to stand your ground, and
after you have done everything, to stand.
Ephesians 6:13

January 23

I will not pass you by. I will not forget you. You are in My path.

My path leads to you, not by you. You are in the road I am traveling on.

You are the reason I am traveling on the road.

Do not think you are mistakenly where you are. I know exactly why you are there.

I am not a God of mistakes.

You have made mistakes which put you on a different, more difficult path than I would have chosen, but because you are Mine, all paths have led to Me.

Sometimes the path seems long and dark but keep going. I am not only at the end of the tunnel bathed in light and love I am beside you through the darkest, most treacherous valleys.

Even though you get discouraged sometimes, I have you in My will. Keep walking, beloved one. I am ever beside you on your path because I love you so much I will never let you walk alone.

Know it in your soul.

Even though I walk through the darkest valley, I will fear no evil, for You are with me; Your rod and Your staff, they comfort me. Surely Your goodness and love will follow me all the days of my life, and I will dwell in the house of the Lord forever.
Psalm 23: 4, 6

January 24

I am here, and I hear your plea. Your timing is right on target and I will answer you.

Know that I always answer, you just may not be expecting the answer I give you.

Faith and the trust it brings are two very important things in our relationship: faith that believes no matter what, faith that doesn't question My answers but humbly submits to My way, and trust that comes from the full belief and acceptance to My way.

There is no other God than Me, beloved one, and I have your back, your front, your sides, your head and your toes! I created those toes, and every one of them is important to Me!

The road I have you on is your personal road to faith and trust that will build an everlasting bridge to Me. This bridge will be strong enough for others to walk on towards Me.

Have faith and trust in Me and the walk I have you on.

Hang on firmly to Me,
as I am your Lifeline, now and forever.

Let us draw near to God with a sincere heart and with the
full assurance that faith brings, having our hearts sprinkled
to cleanse us from a guilty conscience and having our bodies
washed with pure water. Let us hold unswervingly to
the hope we profess, for He Who promised is faithful.
Hebrews 10:22-23

January 25

*W*hether you are sick or whether you are well, I am always with you.

You may not be able to sense My presence at all times, but I am always there. You see, I am in you, as well. Jesus' prayer that we be one as He and I are One was fulfilled on the cross. That means I dwell in you at all times since you have accepted Me into your life.

When you are sick or don't feel well, other feelings are in your body rather than My free-flowing ones. That is when you need to lean on My promises and go out in faith because you know. Not only because of the promises and stories in the Bible, but because of our history together. Yours and Mine.

We have a relationship that will never die because Jesus made it possible.

Now go and rest your weary head and KNOW because you KNOW that I am with you and I will see you through this, too.

All will be well, dear one.
You are safely in My arms and all will be well.

> *I have given them the glory that You gave Me, that they may*
> *be one, as We are one - I in them, and You in Me - so that*
> *they may be brought to complete unity. Then the world*
> *will know that You sent Me and have loved them*
> *even as You have loved Me.*
> *John 17:22-23*

January 26

Every time you close your eyes and think of Me, I am there, in your presence, answering the yearnings of your soul, the yearnings that only I am aware of.

I do not want you to be afraid of the future, to toss and turn, not knowing what to do.

I will guide you, beloved. Do not fear. There is a way mapped out for you and it is the way I have chosen for you to go.

Remember, I am interested in forming your character, not making you comfortable.

What does that mean? This world will not be all rose-covered paths with everything and everyone you want. It will be a path, sometimes long and narrow, that leads you closer to Me.

It's only when you look away from Me that your road takes detours.

But you want the answers more clearly, you say? The answer is there in front of you.

I will never let you down. Just put one foot in front of the other. Take My hand and trust that it's securely in Mine, and that I am leading the way.

Come to Me often during the day. I will show you the answers.
I AM THE ANSWER.

"The Lord Himself goes before you and will be with you;
He will never leave you nor forsake you. Do not be
afraid; do not be discouraged."
Deuteronomy 31:8

January 27

Let Me overwhelm you today with My love. Let Me surround you with the intensity of its reality. It is real.

How could I have possibly given up My Son to be mercilessly beaten and crucified if it were not for love so intense the world could not hold it?

Yet you wander around wondering how there could be a God that is capable of love when you hear of disasters where children are killed, or your own family member suffers and then is taken away from you.

Where is that God of love then? I am beside you, at times carrying you, weeping along with you, showing you My love by allowing the scenario to play out.

I want all the pain and suffering to be over but there is an appointed time when all will come to see and know Good from evil. Then the plan will be complete. Then evil will never be able to raise its head again, and My love will shine over all.

You can't see what I see or know what I know. I am just asking you to trust that as hard as it seems, it is because of Love you are where you are.

So just for today, just for this moment, lay your head on My shoulder, and let Me fill you with My overwhelming love.

It will carry you through . . . I will carry you through.

"Even to your old age and gray hairs, I am He, I am He who
will sustain you. I have made you and I will carry you;
I will sustain you and I will rescue you."
Isaiah 46:4

January 28

Where is your faith, child? Do you doubt Me or My promises when I so lovingly say over and over again how I will take care of you and answer your prayers?

I do not have the problems of the economy you are facing. I have the universe at My disposal. Absolutely everything and anything is possible IF YOU BUT ASK. You have not because you ask not.

Ask, BELIEVING, and I will answer you. I ALWAYS do.

Why do I have to tell you that over and over? Sometimes I get impatient at your unbelief when My daily miracles surround you. Large and small ones happen in your personal life every day.

I know what you need.

Ask, believing, and then thank Me for the answer, showing your faith. Then you can rest peacefully as My carefree child who KNOWS they are so ardently loved and cared for.

Have faith, dear one.
Just ask.

Do not be anxious about anything, but in every situation, by prayer and petition, with thanksgiving, present your requests to God. And the peace of God, which transcends all understanding, will guard your hearts and your minds in Christ Jesus.
Philippians 4:6-7

January 29

Oh, my troubled child, there is so much on your mind this morning. Things which should be laid down at My feet and forgotten, knowing that I will show you the way through each and every one of them.

Today, concentrate on My love, the Love that follows you, surrounds you and guides you.

How can I get through the hard shell you put up around you? Why won't you freely accept the greatest gift ever offered?

The shell you put up cripples you not only for happiness and peace here, but it inhibits your growth in Me. Letting go, laying your pain, insecurity and unbelief down, frees you to openness and peace with Me.

I see you as a child ready to fly, and so willing if you could just lose the shell that holds you down! Lay it at My feet and come fly with Me to the adventure I have planned for you.

How I love and adore you, My child!! Just take a step towards Me. I will show you how.

Lay your shell at the cross.
True joy is waiting for you.

For it is by grace you have been saved, through faith-
and this is not from yourselves,
it is the gift of God.
Ephesians 2:8

January 30

I have the answer you seek, beloved one.

Do not be impatient. Trust Me. I am waiting for you to develop two very important traits: patience and trust. You may think you have achieved them, but you haven't yet.

There is a plan. I have not left you and I never will.

Keep going in the direction you are headed. Keep praying so that I will stay close to you. Trust in Me to guide and direct you.

Again, you have been assured that I answer all of your prayers and that I guide you, yet you are not feeling it now. If you really want to have a clearer knowledge of My guidance, fast and pray. This will also allow you to have a stronger sense of My will for your life.

The answers are there in Me.
Only in Me.

Take delight in the Lord, and He will give you the desires of your heart. Commit your way to the Lord; trust in Him and He will do this: He will make your righteous reward shine like the dawn, your vindication like the noonday sun.
Psalm 37:4-6

January 31

*O*h, beloved child, you come to Me with so many worries and concerns. I already have every one of them covered.

You have not fallen yet. I have not let you. And I will not let you fall in the future, if you stay connected to Me.

All the specifics that you are so worried about are very small in the context of the world. Don't let them overwhelm you. Present them to Me and I will take care of them, all the time guiding and directing you. That is your real need.

You think you need so much, yet it is really just My guidance you need so you will understand how to accomplish what you want. I am there, ready to help you. Always.

This relationship with Me, the benevolent and miraculous care I give you, is not "magic." It was paid for at the cross and has always been available to you, even when you were full of sin.

Since you accepted Christ into your life, I don't see you as a sinner. I see a hurting, wounded child covered with the grace of Christ's love, so ready to be held and cared for.

Come to Me now and let Me fill you with the assurance of My love and care for you. Lay it all at My feet, dear one.

I am always there. Now and forever more.

My son, if you accept My words and store up My commands
within you, then you will understand the fear of the
Lord and find the knowledge of God.
Proverbs 2:1,5

February 01

Surround yourself today with the absolute knowledge of My love and care for you.

Keep coming to Me and presenting your requests to Me. Feel Me envelop you into My arms.

One of My names is El Shaddai. It means I gather you to My bosom. If you close your eyes and imagine it, the sense of My presence will grow more real to you.

One day you will actually be able to really see and feel the tightness of My embrace. Now you must go on faith, a faith that is growing stronger the more we spend time together.

Treasure these stolen moments as much as I do, knowing that drawing closer to Me is the foundation of your faith and the accomplishment of My plan for you.

Come once more and lay your head on the bosom of your El Shaddai.

Let Me fill your being with My peace and joy.

He tends His flock like a Shepherd: He gathers the lambs
in His arms and carries them close to His heart;
He gently leads those that have young.
Isaiah 40:11

February 02

As the clouds float across the sky on a windy day, so My Spirit will enter into and work through you.

I can use you this way, child.
I need to be able to.

I put you in places where I need you to sense the connection with another person. These people I want you to reach are all around you.

My children are hurting, and they need to know about the special relationship I have with you. I want you to share it.

No one can invade our intimacy. It will always be there when you find your quiet place and spend time with me.

Your job is to share My love with others. I will put the hunger in their souls to wonder and pursue, whether right away or in the future.

Don't be afraid. I am always beside you.
Give others the hope you have in Me.

For those who are led by the Spirit of God are the children of God. The Spirit you received does not make you slaves, so that you live in fear again; rather, the Spirit you received brought about your adoption to sonship.
And by him we cry, "Abba, Father."
Romans 8:14-15

February 03

Child of Mine, don't you know how much you are loved? I tell you over and over, yet every day you seem to forget.

When you read this, or really feel My presence close to you, you feel wonderful. Then "life" happens, and the devil is able to get to you and cast doubts in your soul.

Why aren't things perfect? Why are you wanting or why are you hurting?

The more time you spend with Me in our quiet place, the stronger our connection will be. And the stronger the connection, the stronger your armor is against the devil's urgings.

The answer is Me, beloved one.
Me.

Time with Me, throughout the day, remembering and talking to Me. The joy you experience will be something you have never felt before.

The answer is in My everlasting, and undying, REAL love for you.

Praise be to the Lord, for He showed me the wonders of His love when I was in a city under siege. In my alarm I said, "I am cut off from Your sight!" Yet You heard my cry for mercy when I called to You for help. Be strong and take heart, all you who hope in the Lord.
Psalm 31:21-22, 24

February 04

You are My child, My chosen child, yet you act as if it is a duty, not a privilege, to come before Me.

I need you, dear one. I want to see you. I want to hear of your love and devotion. I have given so much to you.

Please receive My gift of love. Come to Me now on bended knee. Reach out your soul to Me. Not only will I take you into My protective arms, I will encapsulate you from danger.

There are rewards of coming to Me: joy, love, and security amidst the hardest of trials. Come to Me now for My yoke is easy and My burden is light.

And joy, dear one.
Joy.

As My peace flows over you, and your burdens loosen, receive My joy in, around and through you. Keep it close. It is our private sign.

No matter what happens, you have Me and I have you.

> *"Take My yoke upon you and learn from Me, for I am gentle and humble in heart, and you will find rest for your souls. For My yoke is easy and My burden is light."*
> *Matthew 11:29-30*

February 05

There are signs all around you in this world I created. Signs of My love, signs of My presence, all around.

You are one of the ones who are aware of it.

What is your role because of that? Keep reading the signs. Look for Me, for I am everywhere.

This knowledge is your hope in what is to those who are not aware, a frightening world.

But you know, dear one, that all will be okay if you choose Me. Mountains may tumble into the sea, floods may rise up around you, but I have you in My pocket.

When fears and loneliness surround you, fly with Me. Take My hand and let Me carry you, if just for a moment, to a place where you are safe and warm and happy.

It is there, so close. Just reach out your hand. Reach out your soul. I am not like the world. I will never let you down. I will never let you go.

Your role here? To love and trust Me through everything no matter how hard. I am the one constant in your life. And believe, My child. Believe I am so close.

All will be okay. Now and always. Just take My hand.

"But blessed is the one who trusts in the Lord, whose confidence is in Him. They will be like a tree planted by the water that sends out its roots by the stream."
Jeremiah 17:7-8

February 06

There is joy all around you, dear one. Joy for you may be at the end of the tunnel, but it is there. Grab hold of it fiercely.

Let the decision of it rule your day.

The decision to have an all-encompassing joy of the knowledge of who you are in Me, of what I have promised you, of what I have waiting for you, of the acceptance of the universe's greatest gift, My Son.

Feel the joy through your pain. Feel it in the midst of your fear.

Joy was always there because there was always a plan, a plan that included you from the very beginning of creation.

It is the hope of the joy of salvation through Jesus Christ, My beloved Son.

This pain and fear you have now are real, dear one. I know it and I feel it with you more than you could know or understand.

Stand with Me, child. There is joy waiting. So much joy to cover the sadness you feel. Joy to cover and seal you as one with Me. Now and always.

You are Mine and I am yours.

Consider it pure joy, my brothers and sisters, whenever you face trials of many kinds, because you know that the testing of your faith produces perseverance. Let perseverance finish its work so that you may be mature and complete, not lacking anything.
James 1:2-4

February 07

This is our time together, dear one. A time where you have chosen to come apart and learn more of My love and sacrifice for you.

Envision the Son of Man coming down a hill, strongly walking. Imagine Him coming and stopping directly in front of you. What does He see?

Does He see a person interested in Him? Or does He see you shift uncomfortably, hoping friends don't see His direct contact with you?

Oh, dear one, this is what it is all about.
This is real.

I am calling you to accept Me and to make a choice. A choice to love Me and to serve Me .

Yes, your friends will know. Whether you tell them, or whether they know it by the change in your activities.

I am calling you. Calling you to make a choice for Me. Take a step towards the Son of Man standing in front of you.

Reach out your hand.

Let the joy and peace flood over you as you feel the warmth of My presence.

Now if we died with Christ, we believe that
we will also live with Him.
Romans 6:8

February 08

Now is the time for you to join together as tight as you can. I need My followers to band together as one.

You will get much relief and comfort from brothers and sisters who are Mine. It doesn't have to be in a church setting or in a prayer group. It can simply be one on one.

To be able to share the good news of My love with another, to encourage them with stories of how I have touched your life and to hear of My actions in theirs will encourage your faith.

I did not create you to be alone. The joining together of My followers will strengthen you. You will find an other-worldly connection that bonds you together as family.

Seek out these people, dear one. Do not stand alone. Share My love and encourage each other.

It is a gift from Me to you.

He died for us so that, whether we are awake or asleep, we
may live together with Him. Therefore encourage
one another and build each other up, just
as in fact you are doing.
I Thessalonians 5:10-11

February 09

*S*tudy to show yourself approved unto Me. Not just for approval, but for a genuine knowledge of Me.

Our relationship is vital, and growth in it comes from letting Me talk directly to you through My Word, so carefully prepared for you and the world many years ago.

Those words are as true now as they were then. The stories you will read in it will captivate your soul. I can, and I want, to work that directly in your life. Please let Me.

Come to My word. Open it and learn from it, of My personality, of My love, of what I want you to be like, and especially of the precious story of My Son Jesus whose death for you and for the world signified the end of the devil's reign.

Oh, come and see that it is a rich bounty of everything important in this world!

And in between the lines, you will sense My presence, My looking over the shoulder of the one I love.

Come and get to know Me better.

The law from Your mouth is more precious to me than
thousands of pieces of silver and gold. May those
who fear You rejoice when they see me, for I
have put my hope in Your word.
Psalm 119:72, 74

February 10

From the sincerity in your heart come words of love and well meaning. I treasure these. Let them flow in abundance. Your praise and your requests come directly up to My mercy seat and I am pleased.

Your words mean so much to Me. Yes, your words to Me. The utterance of them is precious to Me.

Don't ever stop talking to Me, praising and thanking Me, bringing your requests to Me. It deepens our relationship more than anything.

I want to keep you focused on what is above, not on what is going on down below.

Keep your eyes on Me, the Author of your salvation, the Lover of your soul.

I chose you.
Now choose Me.

But I will sing of Your strength, in the morning I will sing of
Your love; for You are my fortress, my refuge in times of
trouble. You are my strength, I sing praise to You.
You, God, are my fortress, my God
on whom I can rely.
Psalm 59:16-17

February 11

Did you know I am sitting beside you now? So close I can feel your breath. I am that real. My presence in your life is that real.

Close your eyes and just know. Know that I am beside you and that My Spirit fills your being.

Jesus made this possible. The death of My Son on the cross enables you to cross over the boundaries of time and space, that we may be one as He and I are one.

Oh, dear one, always love Him! Always serve Him!
Such love you will never find on this earth.

To bear the weight of the sins of all on His magnificent shoulders was the darkest day in the history of time. But it was accomplished at the cross.

One day I will share with you the wonder of joy expressed by living creatures on earth and Heaven when He, My precious Son, rose from the grave in splendor and majesty.

It was over. Accomplished and over.

Share this story, dear one. Share this love. Let your soul thrill to it and dwell in it. Others will know. They need to know.

I am waiting.

For God so loved the world that He gave His one and only
Son, that whoever believes in Him shall not perish
but have eternal life.
John 3:16

February 12

Why are you waiting to do that which I have already encouraged and guided you to do?

Do not wait until everyone agrees with you. If I have already impressed you that way, the time is right.

Stay in My love. Listen closely to the still small voice in your mind. You will know if it is Me talking to you, or the evil one trying to destroy you and the work I have for you by our relationship and by how much time you spend in the Word, in prayer and in communion with Me.

Listen, beloved, listen.

I am the Light that guides your path. You may think you don't know the way, but you will if you are listening to Me. Come apart from the distractions of your life, to our quiet place, and seek My presence, My answers and My guidance.

If you still can't sense it, fast, and pray more, for I am there, dear one. I am ALWAYS with you.

The deeper you get with Me, the more you will sense it.

Deep calls to deep in the roar of Your waterfalls; all Your waves and breakers have swept over me. By day the Lord directs His love, at night His song is with me - a prayer to the God of my life.
Psalm 42:7-8

February 13

Come to Me this morning amidst all the busyness and frustrations of your day. It is a day packed with "important" things for you to do, things which you have determined to be so.

Are they important, dear one?
Are they really so vital as to shut out time between Me and you?

I have to keep reminding you that there is nothing so worthwhile as our morning connection.

I want you to don the armor I have for you. I need you to be fully protected against the evil one. But you must ask for it.

You must ask for Me. Say, "I choose You!!" It is simple enough.

During your most trying and painful moments, bow your head quietly, or lift it up to the heavens and shout, "I CHOOSE YOU!" That choice and declaration loosens the binds of the earth, and power and protection settle over you.

Gear up for this new life with Me. One of the power of My Holy Spirit in your soul.

Lives will be changed. You will be changed.

Therefore let all the faithful pray to You while You may be found; surely the rising of the mighty waters will not reach them. You are my hiding place; You will protect me from trouble and surround me with songs of deliverance.
Psalms 32:6-7

February 14

How do I love you? More than earthly words can explain. More than anything you can even imagine.

Today is a celebrated love day. My celebrated love day happened on Calvary years ago. There will never be another act more deserving of love than what was accomplished that day on the cross.

Many people have died saving others' lives, but never one more undeserving than Jesus. He didn't just die for you. He died carrying all of your sins, and the sins of the entire world.

He was the blameless Lamb, separated from Me, mercilessly tortured and murdered so that you and so many others could receive eternal life.

Crucified, so that the evil one would finally be conquered.

Do you have someone who is your valentine today? Or have you lost them? Either way, take comfort in knowing that the greatest Love of your life is with you now, right beside you.

You are My beloved one. Today, celebrate our love, and your future together with Me. Keep your eyes looking up.

Share our love with others. It is the one true love people's hearts cry out for.

Never be lonely, dear one. I am beside you now.

> *"Let the beloved of the Lord rest secure in Him, for He shields him all day long, and the one the Lord loves rests between His shoulders."*
> *Deuteronomy 33:12*

February 15

How bright the day starts out when you are with Me!

Your reaction to things that happen are so much easier for you. No problem is so big that together we cannot conquer it.

You are a conqueror, My hidden soldier, a lasting witness of My love, and you just thought you had a regular day in front of you!

We have much to do together, dear one. Much to do in My field.

Don't let that statement overwhelm you. I just need you to trust Me and let me guide you through it. You won't even know when most of what I do occurs.

People are watching you and hearing you. They can sense My Holy Spirit and My love through you.

We have a story to tell. A story that will bring salvation, hope and love to a lost generation.

Will you join Me today?

Take My hand. Enjoy the journey.

No, in all these things we are more than conquerors
through Him who loved us.
Romans 8:37

February 16

*W*orship Me, My love. Sing songs to Me.

No matter how good or bad your voice is, to Me it is pure joy to listen to you praise My name.

The song may be one of your choosing, or in a church with many others, but it is very precious to hear you praise My name in this way.

Don't just mouth the words that are on the page or screen. Really feel them. I do. And the heavenly noise floats up to Heaven and fills the courts with praise. Thank you, dear child.

You are Mine and I am yours.
Thank you for choosing Me.

Your decision is made possible because of My dear Son's death on the cross. There is much to rejoice of and much to sing about.

And your Heavenly Father Who loves you so much, is listening.

Praise the Lord with the harp; make music to Him on the ten-stringed lyre. Sing to Him a new song; play skillfully, and shout for joy. For the word of the Lord is right and true; He is faithful in all He does.
Psalm 33:2-4

February 17

All things are possible through Me. Do not fear.

You have nothing to be afraid of when you love and trust Me because My love for you is overwhelming.

Just swim in it.

Lay back and envision floating in a sea of love, so pure and buoyant. You are free from the cares of this world, from its pains and sorrow. You are surrounded by ministering angels who watch your every step.

As you rise up from your imaginary bed of water, keep that feeling with you because I am with you.

I will never leave or desert you.

You are a free-flying bird with direction and ease. How the wind responds to the pressure of your wings to keep you soaring high and free! I am the wind under your wings enabling you to fly free and high.

Come out from under your fear, for with Me all things are possible.

You and Me. Me and you.

But those who hope in the Lord will renew their strength.
They will soar on wings like eagles; they will run and not
grow weary; they will walk and not be faint.
Isaiah 40:31

February 18

When the cold winter weather whips around you, know I am your safe, warm spot. Keep searching. You will find Me and relax into the warmth of My shelter and comfort.

Imagine you are the coldest you have ever been. You are standing out in the middle of a frozen field with nothing but snow and ice around you.

What do you do? Do you stay where you are? No. You keep walking until you find a warm place to be comfortable and cozy.

Your daily life is like that. You are now standing out in that frozen field. Your faith is frozen. Our relationship is frozen.

Keep walking towards the warmth and light. Do not think it might be easier to stop where you are and live your life like that. Many people's souls are just like that.

I am calling you to the warmth, to the light of My love and countenance.

Such joy as you lay on the pillow of faith and you pull the sheet of hope and the blanket of love around you until you are safely and snugly in My arms!

Make the decision to keep walking, loved one.
Walk towards Me and the light of My love and comfort.

Indeed, if you call out for insight and cry aloud for
understanding, and if you look for it as for silver and search
for it as for hidden treasure, then you will understand
the fear of the Lord and find the knowledge of God.
Proverbs 2:3-5

February 19

Write down the thoughts I send to you today. They are things I am impressing on your mind. These thoughts can be read during the day, to strengthen and encourage you.

When I created you, I gave you a mind to seek and worship Me because I want to keep you close to Me.

But how do you do that? By coming to Me in the morning and committing your life to Me daily, by reading My Word, and then by listening to My gentle urgings throughout the day.

When you write your thoughts down, it not only helps you to remember them, it helps to increase your faith.

My Word is true, and I will never let you down.

The words of love and guidance will be a source of comfort when you are low or need assurance of My presence in your life.

Listen, dear one.
I am the still small voice ever in and around you, and always with you.

Now choose life, so that you and your children may live and that you may love the Lord your God, listen to His voice, and hold fast to Him. For the Lord is your life.
Deuteronomy 30:19-20

February 20

Do you feel like you are the child of the King of the universe? When others tout the importance of a person they might know, or have met, do you tell them about your lineage and how I, the Ruler and Creator of all, chose you to be My child, perfectly forming you to be exactly how I wanted you to be?

What a privilege you have! And your growing connection to Me is proof of that privilege. Do you take it for granted?

Oh, the terrible price that had to be paid for it! The awesome weight, and yet the joy of it, should overwhelm your life. It must never be taken for granted.

Isn't that where you want to be, beloved? Wouldn't you rather be with Me, and talk about our real relationship, or with those whose sense of importance stems from their connection to someone who lives and breathes and dies, and who has garnered temporary and fleeting fame on this earth somehow?

What you know is that you can introduce them to the most important relationship in their life. One that will determine not just bragging rights, but eternal life, and the love, support and joy that our daily relationship brings.

So, next time you hear about that "important" so and so, don't hesitate to tell them about the Master of the universe, your Friend, your beloved Father . . . Me.

See what great love the Father has lavished on us, that we should be called children of God! And that is what we are!
I John 3:1

February 21

Your mind is far away as you think about how to solve all your problems. Don't you know it is with Me that your problems will be solved?

Bring them to Me, and thank Me, having faith that I will answer, and then have peace because you have placed them in My hands. Keep remembering this promise throughout the day.

Yes, there are things you need to do, but I will let you know what and when.

How sad the world of people who don't know Me and what I bring when they make the choice for Me! Tell them, dear one. Tell them about the many joys of coming to Me. Don't keep it to yourself.

Learn to come to Me with your whole mind. Put your focus on Me. Lay your head back and close your eyes.

Say: "I choose you, Lord. Please help me today."

I will be there, dear one. I am with you now. Now and always. Just call out My name.

I keep asking that the God of our Lord Jesus Christ, the
glorious Father, may give you the Spirit of wisdom
and revelation, so that you may know Him better.
Ephesians 1:17

February 22

As snow falls so tenderly from the heavens, so My love gently falls on you, caressing you with little drops of love notes to let you know you are cared for.

Oh, so gently they land on you and around you, little stimuli to encourage and guide you until you are totally surrounded and covered. Do not shake off this wonderful cascade. Let these little messages from Me absorb into your body.

Most of the world runs quickly and they don't feel or hear Me. If they could remove the dark glass in front of them and see My beloved ones as I do, they would see the snow flurries of love and guidance falling all over you, and then they would look at their plain, ungifted existence and want what you have.

The enemy sees it, beloved one. He sees, and because of it, he knows you are set apart. He may wreak havoc on the world, but he may never enter your "space" if you stay close to Me.

So, no matter what the temperature is outside, close your eyes and stand with your arms outstretched.

Feel My loving snowflakes falling on you and around you, just a little of the joy I share with you.

Though you have not seen Him, you love Him; and even
though you do not see Him now, you believe in Him
and are filled with an inexpressible and glorious joy.
I Peter 1:8

February 23

Ever since you first came to Me, I have filled you with a longing for My presence. My Holy Spirit has entered in and found a home in your soul.

Every day you say, "I choose You!", He settles in to guide and direct you, prompting you to say or do things that are in My plan for your life.

He is My secret tool, the One everyone who comes to Me needs and receives. He prepares the heart of the most hardened atheist and the greatest skeptic and moves them to wonder at My creation, to have guilt for their actions, and to seek Me in the crucified and risen Christ.

He is the beginning of salvation in a sinner's heart,
My right hand.

You don't need to know or study much about Him. Just know He is there inside you when you ask for My presence and guidance.

The team of "Us" have got you covered, My beloved one.

You never need to fear.

And hope does not put us to shame, because God's love has been poured out into our hearts through the Holy Spirit, who has been given to us.
Romans 5:5

February 24

*A*re you facing a "lion's den" today? Are you afraid of the outcome?

You never need to be afraid, dear one, for I am with you. If you ask, the whole Wonder Team surrounds you, not just the three of us "Big Guys", but a score of angels.

We are your Defense Team, a mightier one never seen.
Nothing can prevail against us.

Watch for the miracles to happen. One you never even thought about. So, walk into your situation with your head held high.

Or is it pain so unbearable you think you can't handle it? That same Wonder Team is there, surrounding and comforting you.

There is joy and peace on the other side.

You will never be alone, My beloved child, never. I have promised you that, and I have shown you that. Your deepest thoughts and fears are in the front of My mind. My pain for them and for you is greater than what you feel. I understand and I know.

Together we can conquer and overcome anything.
There is joy on the other side.

"No weapon forged against you will prevail, and you will
refute every tongue that accuses you. This is the heritage
of the servants of the Lord, and this is their
vindication from me," declares the Lord.
Isaiah 54:17

February 25

*D*id I not show you My love in a direct way recently? Do you still continue to doubt not only My presence in your life, but My very existence, as well?

I know what lingers in the back of your mind, and it hurts, beloved one. The devil will send you these types of messages constantly.

When you stay tuned into Me, you shut them quickly out. But when you are weak, you allow them to linger, causing a deadly, cancerous growth that if unchecked, will take over your body and your mind. Beware of these things. Shut them out. Shut him out.

He is the author of sin and pain, yet the wily one comes bearing gifts, looking kind, compassionate and wise. He robs people of their faith and trust in Me.

Consider the reality of what is going on. I love you more than you can understand, even sending My Son to die a cruel death on the cross so We would overcome evil and I could have you with Me. Yet you are listening to the one who started this pain and suffering thousands of years ago and who only wants to separate us so that you will die. He wants to take as many people with him as he can.

You have chosen Me. When one of those negative thoughts come to your mind, immediately shut them out and say, "I choose You, Lord!"

The stakes are high, and the battle is very real. Be ever aware.

"My prayer is not that you take them out of the world but that you protect them from the evil one."
John 17:15

February 26

It was Me all along: the one you envisioned being beside you, sitting and walking with you. I'm not saying you do not or will never have an earthly partner to walk or sit beside you, but that I have always been there. And when you dreamt of "the one", it was Me.

I want you to know, particularly today, how much I love and adore you. I feel the heaviness in your heart.

Come and let Me hold you against My chest. I will be your El Shaddai today, pushing the cares of the world away and just for the moment, our moment, I can make you forget all the pain and sadness in this life because I know how frightened you are.

Oh, dear one, please know that although this door seems closed, it is not.

Just trust Me during this time. You thought you were on the right path with your plans. It will come in My time. Trust Me for the answers. I want you to take care of other things first.

Don't be frightened, dear one. Trust in Me. You are not alone, now or ever. I will not let you fall.

Your burdens are heavy, but My arms are strong. Strong enough to create the universe, and strong enough to carry it in My arms. Strong enough to hold and comfort the child I have chosen as Mine.

We will get through this, too, beloved one.
Just hang on. The ride is not over. It is just beginning.

> *Those who know Your name trust in You, for You, Lord,*
> *have never forsaken those who seek You.*
> *Psalm 9:10*

February 27

I have an investment in you, such a huge investment in you. One of time, love and sacrifice.

You are familiar with the Sacrifice, but not the pain and suffering behind it. The pain you feel over losses, even the loss of a beloved child cannot compare.

Jesus was a sinless child Who chose to love even those who reviled Him, those who drove the nails into His hands, those who tore His flesh with whips with metal barbs at the end. He allowed the separation from Me during that time so that He could bear all the weight of the world's sin on Him, the sinless One. He knew there was no other way to conquer evil than for the sinless One to bear everyone else's sin.

And I chose to let My precious Son, of whom I was so proud, endure it. I had to separate Myself from Him in order to allow it to happen. I could have destroyed the whole world at that moment, but Our love for you and humanity was so intense that I chose to allow My Child, My only begotten Son, to die, so that one day you could live in a sinless, perfect world where all sadness will be gone.

Yes, I have an investment in you. One that I will always cherish and protect. Look for the nail scars. Search for them. They will always be there as a reminder of My investment in you.

But He was pierced for our transgressions, He was crushed
for our iniquities; the punishment that brought us peace
was on Him, and by His wounds we are healed.
Isaiah 53:5

February 28

Courage and joy: two words I ask you to carry inside you throughout the most difficult circumstances; the darkest times when you don't understand My answers to your prayers.

I am beside you at those moments, even closer than I was when you were carefree.

Sometimes the devil does things that I have to allow so that this world will run its course and good will play out against evil. Other times I put roadblocks up just when you thought things were okay to grow your trust in Me, to develop your character.

Lean on Me in either circumstance. I am your constant guide. I will never put you in a position where the pain will be too great to bear.

Look up, My precious child. Let Me see your face. Let Me fill you with the courage and joy to face any and all circumstances.

Courage and joy.

Remember those two words today as you go out in the world. Find them in Me.

You will go out in joy and be led forth in peace; the
mountains and hills will burst into song before you,
and all the trees of the field will clap their hands.
This will be for the Lord's renown, for an everlasting
sign, that will endure forever.
Isaiah 55: 12-13b

March 01

How many times I have called you to Me! How many times I have lovingly comforted you, yet you keep turning your back on Me.

Yes, you are here with Me now, but during the day, am I with you? Do you think of Me? Send up praises or requests to Me?

I want so much more from you, beloved one. We have just begun our journey together, the only journey worth taking in this life because it leads to Me and our eternal life together.

Keep your eyes focused on Me. The journey will not be easy or painless, but it is ours, well planned out before the beginning of time.

It is important for you to realize how vital your role is to Me and how much you are needed. Not only do I need your love, but others love and need who you are, too. I have groomed you through all the hills and valleys to be just who you are. You may not understand the picture now, but one day all will become clear.

Stay connected to Me today, all day. Think of Me. Praise Me. Send Me your requests.

The Lover of your soul is longing to lead you on our journey together. I have great things planned for you, dear one.

One step at a time.

The Lord makes firm the steps of the one who delights in Him; though he may stumble, he will not fall, for the Lord upholds him with His hand.
Psalm 37:23-24

March 02

*H*ow great the plans I have for you! If I were to unveil them now, you would shudder. Never forget that I created you, and I know exactly what you are capable of doing.

I see you rising higher and higher in the work I have planned, reaching out to others in your own simple way. The corporate CEO is just as important to Me as the mom at home raising future leaders for Me.

Each of My chosen ones is a leader, getting ready for battle. Who do you battle? You battle evil and sin, the devil himself. The people he influences seem strong, and they do heartless things to others. But they are really weak inside, and they are scared. Scared of death and of their lives not being important on this earth, satan's realm. He twists them like mannequins.

Most of these people are admired here because they seem important, but their time will soon be over, and they will be forgotten. They will face me all too soon.

Is there hope for them? Only I know. Don't stop praying for them. Live your life for Me. One day you will look back at how I have led you in this life, and you will be amazed at how far we have come.

My little child became a leader for Me!

> *Therefore, since we are surrounded by such a great cloud of witnesses, let us throw off everything that hinders and the sin that so easily entangles. And let us run with perseverance the race marked out for us, fixing our eyes on Jesus, the pioneer and perfecter of faith.*
> *Hebrews 12:1-2*

March 03

Take My hand. Walk with Me to the other side of your grief, of your fears. Be a child again, walking beside Me . . . trusting Me.

You never used to worry about where you were going when you were a child. Someone would drive the car and you sat in the back waiting for the arrival, and you didn't know where you were going.

Then, you didn't have a choice in trusting the outcome. You simply needed to go along with your parents obediently.

Now you have a choice to make.

You are an adult, and you think for yourself. I am asking you to go to a place where you don't know where you are going, or where you will end up.

I am asking you to put your hand in Mine, and walk with Me, keeping your focus on Me and on our conversation, not on where I am taking you. Be that child again.

Trust Me, My beloved child.

I have you in the palm of My hand. Trust Me to lead you places higher and better than you had planned.

Walk with Me, beloved one.
Take My hand.

By faith Abraham, when called to go to a place he would
later receive as his inheritance, obeyed and went, even
though he did not know where he was going.
Hebrews 11:8

March 04

When you take My hand through the crises you are facing, I am so close to you. I am beside you in your decision-making process.

I know you are laden with fear.

To the world you seem strong,
but I know My child inside and out.

I long to have you turn it all over to Me to receive the peace only I can give, the peace I can freely bestow upon you. This gift will bless you in so many ways.

Peace in a believer's life encourages joy, and even strengthens the immune system to help with your health.

This gift is free to you, but it was not free for Us. It is only because of Jesus' death on the cross that all this is made available to you.

Please accept Him, and through Him, Me,
and the peace together We bring.

Take My hand, dear one.
All is ok now.

Great peace have those who love Your law,
and nothing can make them stumble.
Psalm 119:165

March 05

I have opened a new world before you.

I am just starting to show you the plan I have for you. It is different than what you thought, but I am in the middle, beginning and end of it all.

Are you excited?
A new path to travel on!
You just thought your dreams were over!

Yes, you still have problems now, and your problems will never stop. They are how I keep you close to Me, helping you learn to depend upon Me daily.

Remember the courage and joy I asked you to have during your time of despair. Keep those feelings.

I am pleased with you, dear one. You have shown yourself to be faithful to Me in many trials, and although you didn't understand why these things happened, I never let you down.

You are still here with Me, and I with you. So open up your heart and your mind. I have many wonderful things in store for you.

Stay close. Always stay close.

Give me understanding, so that I may keep Your law and obey it with all my heart. Direct me in the path of Your commands, for there I find delight.
Psalm 119:34-35

March 06

*Y*our heart is heavy this morning, loved one. Don't be scared. I have you in the palm of My hand.

I will never let you go, and I will never let you fall.

The world, as you know it, is changing. The world, as I know it, never changes. Everything that happens has been planned since time immemorial.

Hold out your hand. I will take it and guide you. When you get frightened, remember where you are and Who is with you.

Think of the scriptures of the Shepherd leading the lamb. I am the Shepherd and you are My lamb. Though you walk through the valley of death, you will not be afraid, for you are with Me.

I make you lie down in green pastures. Stay here awhile in the green pasture and let Me enfold you with My peace and love.

When you are ready, take My hand and let Me carry your load through to the other side.

Just trust Me, My child.
I will not lead you astray.

He makes me lie down in green pastures, He leads me beside
quiet waters. Even though I walk through the darkest valley,
I will fear no evil, for You are with me;
Psalm 23:2, 4

March 07

*D*oes your world seem to be falling down around you?

I have a better plan for you than what you can see or know. Please do not be afraid. You are not walking in uncharted territory. You are walking on the path I have planned for you.

Step out of the security of your earthly knowledge and into faith in Me. The time is here and now. No more waiting.

Just free fall into the unknown limits of faith. I will catch you and together we will fly.

Take that step of faith, beloved. The rewards are limitless. Don't ever be afraid.

I did not put you here to rest in your own security. My walk for you is going to be one of adventure, much different than what you might have thought before.

Your security is in Me, and Me alone.

Together we can walk through anything!!

Never be lacking in zeal, but keep your spiritual fervor,
serving the Lord. Be joyful in hope, patient in
affliction, faithful in prayer.
Romans 12:11-12

March 08

$\mathcal{I}$ have given you so much helpful information in the Bible, passages which I draw you to to give you comfort and to direct your path. Use them often and keep our lines of communication open.

I know you don't know what to do. I do, however, and will continue guiding you.

Do not give up, now or ever.

You have consecrated yourself to Me to use for My good.

Just hang on, beloved one. I will guide you.

Seek counsel of your earthly Christian mentors, but always come back to Me for the final word. They see things from earthly standpoints. I ask you to step out in faith.

I will show you a sign, dear one.
You will know. Stay close to Me.

I have come into the world as a light, so that no one
who believes in Me should stay in darkness.
John 12:46

March 09

*O*h, how I long to put My arms around you and comfort you!

No matter how many times I reassure you of My love, when you go out into the world, the devil and his entourage barrage you at every turn. Your thoughts turn away from Me, and insecurity and depression set in.

Am I really right beside you? Will I really guide you like I say?

When you are in our private place, you have that assurance, but when you leave to face the world, you start to doubt.

Like any soldier who has fought a long battle and gets to come home to renew their strength, come back into My arms and I will strengthen you there.

All your fears will subside when you are at My side.

Oh, My dear one, it breaks My heart to have you keep doubting Me. The price Jesus and I paid for our connection was too high to ever give up on you.

Come back now to our quiet place.
I am there, waiting.

For just as we share abundantly in the sufferings of Christ,
so also our comfort abounds through Christ.
2 Corinthians 1:5

March 10

I know you, dear one. I know every hair on your head. I know when you rise, when you sit and when you lie down.

Those are the visual things I see about you. More importantly, I know the very inside of you. I know your fears, your doubts. I hear the things you say, or the things you are afraid to say.

And yet, I love you even more.

From the foundation of the world I planned to have you with Me. I created you to love and serve Me, and to be with Me.

You are not a mistake, an evolutionary happening. No, dear one, far from it. You were planned.

I personally formed you in your mother's womb.

Because you cannot see Me does not mean I love you any less, or that I will take care of you any less. I see you and I know you from the inside out, and that makes Me love you even more for all the crazy little things that make you you.

Be secure in that, for:

I . . . KNOW . . . YOU

For You created my inmost being, You knit me
together in my mother's womb.
Psalm 139:13

March 11

How many times have you seen birds fly from branch to branch? They alight for a while, sing out their praises, and then fly off again.

Their lives are very busy. It's hard for you to figure out their lives, but they have a very special purpose in My creation. Just one of their purposes is to be appreciated by humans.

I made many of them to be brilliant and beautiful. Their songs fill the air with joyful praise to Me.

They are My gifts to you. Watch them. Listen to them. Study their carefree joy.

Their little lives are not easy. They must stay constantly busy in order to survive. And yet not one of them will fall unless I know it.

As I care for these little creatures, I care even more for you.

Sing a song of joy and praise to Me now. It will lift your spirits as you go about your day.

Remember the lowly sparrow, dear one. I love you even more. So very much more.

Are not two sparrows sold for a penny? Yet not one of them will fall to the ground outside your Father's care. And even the very hairs of your head are all numbered. So, don't be afraid; you are worth more than many sparrows.
Matthew 10:29-31

March 12

I am the Good Shepherd.

I lovingly guide you through paths of darkness and turmoil, never letting go of your hand. You never need to be afraid.

Sometimes you stop and look down when you don't understand or can't see the end. Don't do that, My child. Keep looking up, grasping tightly to My hand.

You have My promise.

My promise is not that you will live a happy, carefree life, but that I will always be with you, now and forever, drawing you close to Me through whatever the evil one throws at you.

Whether it is through the loss of a loved one, the pain of rejection, fear of the future, or the pain of sickness, I am with you through it all.

I feel every single thing you are going through and long to have you weep, together with Me, in My arms.

Let Me shelter you now. In Me you will find true security. A true shelter in the time of storm.

Hold My hand. You can do it.
We will get through this. You and Me, Me and you.
Now and always.

"I am the Good Shepherd; I know My sheep and My sheep know Me - just as the Father knows Me and I know the Father - and I lay down My life for the sheep."
John 10:14-15

March 13

*D*ear child, I am here.

You can't see Me yet, and you don't understand why I am taking you through this dark valley.

I cannot tell you My reasons now, but I can tell you that you are not alone. I see your anguish. I feel your pain and I am right beside you on this. We will get through it together. Do not doubt that for one minute.

You will have whatever you need at the time you really need it. Is it strength? Or courage? Or finances?

Wait with Me. Don't tear your heart out. Wait with Me. You will see and understand one day.

Lay back and let Me hold you now. Relax into My arms and feel the peace overwhelm you.

You are not alone, dear one.

You are My beloved, chosen child
whom I will never leave and
never forsake.

Be strong and courageous. Do not be afraid or terrified
because of them, for the LORD your God goes with you;
He will never leave you nor forsake you.
Deuteronomy 31:6

March 14

*D*o you wonder at the upheaval of these times? Surely My coming is nigh!

You are a creature of faith and love, and you don't understand why horrors in the world happens.

Aren't I a God of love? How can I let this happen?

Times like these were foretold of in the Bible, "in the last days". This sinful world is quickly coming to an end, My child, and I need you to focus on the reality of our relationship. It is the only real thing that matters.

I have always had a plan for you. You were in that plan before the beginning of the world. It is a plan of love and salvation for all mankind. It comes down to the strongest personal love between Me and each of My children that has ever been known.

It is not a love that promises peace and happiness on this earth. I do promise you everlasting peace and happiness in Heaven with Me, however.

Focus on Me, My love. Reach out for My hand. Do not fear.
My coming is closer than you think.

For the Lord Himself will come down from heaven, with a loud command, with the voice of the archangel and with the trumpet call of God, and the dead in Christ will rise first. After that, we who are still alive and are left will be caught up together with them in the clouds to meet the Lord in the air. And so we will be with the Lord forever. Therefore encourage one another with these words.
I Thessalonians 4:16-18

March 15

You are scared. You are tired. Hang on to Me. Don't let go. You need Me now more than ever.

Did I plan it that way? Part of it I planned and part of it happened because you have fallen into the snare of the devil, or disaster and pain has happened around you.

There is only one real thing you need. It is Me. Everything else you think you need falls short of our relationship.

Don't keep trying to fight. You are not walking alone. I am filled with pain when I see the tiredness in your face and body. Lay your head on My chest and feel the joy rise up as I fill you with My love and protection.

Everything will be okay because you have chosen Me. I already chose you when I created you.

All it takes is faith and strength.
You will find both in My open arms.

For we do not have a high priest who is unable to empathize with our weaknesses, but we have One Who has been tempted in every way, just as we are, yet He did not sin. Let us then approach God's throne of grace with confidence, so that we may receive mercy and find grace to help us in our time of need.
Hebrews 4:15-16

March 16

Spring is right around the corner. With spring comes newness of life, new beginnings and joy as the earth unfolds her tender beauty; beauty that was always there, but in hibernation through the winter months.

Earth sighs with relief as this season comes, and with it I am able to show you the beauty of My creation all over again: new leaves, new flowers, new baby birds, new life.

May I ask you for a new commitment to Me this new spring? Shed the layer of pain and sorrow from the winter of your life. Celebrate the newness of spring by coming to Me as a new creation, full of trust and love.

You have been washed white with the blood of Christ. You are My innocent child.

Take My hand and we will walk together in trust and joy.

I have so much in store for My beloved child!!

Brothers and sisters, I do not consider myself yet to have taken hold of it. But one thing I do: forgetting what is behind and straining toward what is ahead, I press on toward the goal to win the prize for which God has called me heavenward in Christ Jesus.
Philippians 3:13-14

March 17

Everything that happens in your life is pre-ordained by Me. I knew what you would do, how you would react, and what would be the result.

Many things happen because of your actions, many things happen because the devil wants to cause those I love pain, and many more things happen because I want to develop you into the person I created you to be.

So, do not be discouraged when everything around you seems to be falling apart, when you feel like you are falling apart. I knew it was going to happen before time began. Letting go and taking My hand is the best way to take care of it.

Putting years on your life by stressing over it all may seem the only way out, but it is not, My love.

I am the way out and the way through, your pain and depression.

I am ready for anything you throw My way. I will catch you and hold you until you have no more tears, until I can stand you back up, straight and strong, full of My wisdom and power.

Don't resist. Just bow your head and say, "I choose You, Lord. Help me!"

I am here now.

All the days ordained for me were written in your book before one of them came to be. How precious to me are your thoughts, God! How vast is the sum of them! Were I to count them, they would outnumber the grains of sand-when I awake, I am still with you.
Psalm 139:16-18

March 18

*A*re you listening, dear one?

Can you hear My voice through all the noise and distraction of your daily life?

You are confused and wonder what you should do. I have been trying to tell you, but you allow the world to get in between My direct messages to you.

Go to your quiet place and lay open your heart before Me. Empty your soul to hear the still small voice. The answer is unfolding before you.

The help you need, the answers you need, are all right there. Reach out and grab your future.

With Me your future will be bright.

Keep looking upward with faith. Do not look down or you will stumble and fall. With your eyes kept steadily on Me, you will never lose your way.

I have the help and guidance you need for your journey, for our journey together.

Grab My hand and take your first step.
I will help you take the second.

For this God is our God for ever and ever;
He will be our guide even to the end.
Psalm 48:14

March 19

$\mathcal{O}$h, the mysteries of this life! Mysteries so deep and rich only I can unfold them for you.

The "intelligent" and renowned scientists of your generation seek relentlessly for the answer, but without Me there is no answer.

I am at the beginning, middle and end of every scientific equation ever presented. They think they are so smart, they have it all figured out . . . or not!

They are unaware of the simplicity of your beautiful faith, and the relationship we have because of it, allowing you to trust Me to receive the magnificent gifts I have given you. The scientists want to discount My gifts of love and figure out how time and evolution created things on their own.

You have accepted the wonderful, miraculous bodies and earth I made, My precious one. One day you will see how it all unfolded so many years ago, and how it is still unfolding every day in the beauty of new life.

It doesn't take mighty, brilliant minds.
It takes simple faith in Me.

This is what the Lord says, the Holy One of Israel, and its Maker: "Concerning things to come, do you question Me about My children, or give Me orders about the work of My hands? It is I who made the earth and created mankind on it."
Isaiah 45:11-12

March 20

*Y*es, I am with you, always and forever.

There is not one time where you were left alone to face earthly battles on your own. I promised you early on that I would never leave you or forsake you, and I have kept My promise.

I love to be near you, dear one. I love to watch you as you rise in the morning, start the day and then all throughout the day as you face many challenges head-on.

I am the doting Father who cannot get too much of His beloved child.

How can you really know and sense that? By communion with Me. Daily minute-by-minute communion with Me.

Let Me enter your soul every morning and adorn you with love and protection. And the armor to protect you from all evil.

Stand tall, My soldier.
We have much to do.

Cast your cares on the Lord and He will sustain you;
He will never let the righteous be shaken.
Psalm 55:22

March 21

The Bible is a storehouse of everything you need to know on this earth.

Don't be mistaken by thinking that I don't want you to learn anything else. It is important, too. But as a guidance for your life on earth and for eternal life, there is none other.

It is the story of Me.

Its pages are rich, and full of the travails of My people for thousands of years, ending with the magnificent story of salvation played out through Jesus' life and ministry, death and resurrection.

Open this most important book, dear one. Let its pages teach you. Through it I can talk directly to you.

Just start reading.
I will guide you.

Your statutes are wonderful; therefore I obey them.
The unfolding of Your words gives light;
it gives understanding to the simple.
Psalm 119:129-130

March 22

I want you to start this day with joy, dear one. With courage and joy.

Rise up with purpose for the mission I have given you. Everything will unfold before you as you go. Step by step.

Look into My face. Do you see anything there that will cause you to doubt My presence and guidance? You will find only love encouraging you to reach our goals together.

Perhaps that goal is as simple as getting through this day. Don't look away. Keep your eyes focused on Me, the Author and Perfecter of your faith.

The love you see will fill every pore of your body, enveloping you with calm and peace amid the storm.

I will never leave you or forsake you.

So, whether it is getting through today, or climbing great mountains to shout out My love through the valleys, I will be there to help and encourage you.

You are Mine and I am yours.
Now and forevermore.

Be strong and courageous. Do not be afraid or terrified
because of them, for the Lord your God goes with you;
He will never leave you nor forsake you.
Deuteronomy 31:6

March 23

Fling yourself at the feet of the mercy seat. I know your situation. You must remember this is all about timing. My timing.

Yes, I know, and I care. And it causes Me to hurt.

Listen to the still, small voice. I will guide and direct you. Through Me you will know the way.

I am all merciful and all powerful. Come before Me now and test and see that I am good.

You are My beloved child in whom I have placed a ministry. It may be different than what you thought it was going to be, but My yoke is easy, and My burden is light.

Come, take My hand and walk with Me. Let Me tell you the stories of men and women I raised up, just like you.

I love you, dear one.
I am proud of how far you have come.

Don't let go of My hand. Cry for mercy.

I will be there.

"Take My yoke upon you and learn from Me, for I am gentle and humble in heart, and you will find rest for your souls. For My yoke is easy and My burden is light."
Matthew 11:29-30

March 24

$\mathcal{P}$ut your hand in the hand of the One Who parted the waters, Who created the seas and the fish that teem in them. Put your hand in the hand of the One Who laughed, Who cried, and Who lived on this earth.

Put your hand in the hand of the One Who gave His Son to die for you on the cross, Whose blood poured out on the ground, cleansing the permanent title of sin on earth, enabling you to have this relationship with Me.

Put your hand in the hand of the One Whose love for you was before time began, Who ultimately formed every inch of you.

Oh, beloved one, do not let time pass you by. I am waiting, with My hand outstretched. Come with Me and let Me take you to a place of rest and peace, where you have never been before.

Our time together is precious, much more than you realize.

Do not delay.
Only love awaits.

I have been crucified with Christ and I no longer live, but Christ lives in me. The life I now live in the body, I live by faith in the Son of God, Who loved me and gave Himself for me.
Galatians 2:20

March 25

There is no God greater than I. I created the heavens and the earth. I hung each star in the sky. I placed each tiny tendril of hair on your head, and above each eye.

You, like the universe, are My own creation. I made you to be just who you are. I fill you with a sense of joy and wonderment as you gaze upon the beauty of My creation. You were born to love and praise Me, to honor and serve Me, yet you are filled with fear.

It's not about this life, loved one. It is about an eternal life with Me, your Father, your El Shaddai.

I do not humble Myself for anything, yet I gave My precious Son to die on the cross for you to be able to be one with Me. I reach out to you constantly, guiding and protecting you so that you don't fall into the trap of the evil one.

satan will go down into the fiery pit one day, beloved, and all the earth will sing in its new freedom. And the child I kept with Me will sit at My feet and sing My praise. Such joy will fill the heavens! What a glorious day that will be!

Hang on, dear one.
That is what this life is about.

When I consider Your heavens, the work of Your fingers, the moon and the stars, which You have set in place, what is mankind that You are mindful of them, human beings that You care for them? You have made them a little lower than the angels and crowned them with glory and honor.
Psalm 8:3-5

March 26

Do you hear Me calling you? I call you often, hoping you will be quiet enough to hear My voice and listen to My heeding.

I am calling you to step out of your comfort zone and be a witness for Me. I am calling you to greatness you may think impossible.

Nothing is impossible with Me.

Listen to My voice, dear one. It is all around you.

Turn off the TV, the radio, the computer. Go to your quiet place in your Bible. Read stories of My love and sacrifice for you and My other children and then listen. Listen as I call out to you. It will sound small at first, but in time you will learn to be more perceptive.

Imagine Me sitting beside you. Write the thoughts that come to your mind as you focus on Me.

I love you, child, and I long to draw ever nearer to you.
Learn to listen. It will lead you to the greatness I desire of you.

You and Me, Me and you.

We ourselves heard this voice that came from heaven when we were with Him on the sacred mountain. We also have the prophetic message as something completely reliable, and you will do well to pay attention to it, as to a light shining in a dark place, until the day dawns and the morning star rises in your hearts
2 Peter 1:18-19

March 27

Today, I want you to put one foot in front of the other to do the job I have asked for you to do. I know what it is.

Take tiny steps if you are afraid. Just keep moving towards the goal.

I am with you, in you, and around you every step of the way to give you courage and joy at every corner.

Don't stop. Just keep moving.

You will never arrive. That may be upsetting to hear but the work I have given you will never be done. If you think you have arrived and settle into comfort, you will become complacent and that is worth nothing to Me.

Only think about the one or two steps you will take today.

Hold My hand.
I will be with you.

I press on toward the goal to win the prize for which God has called me heavenward in Christ Jesus.
Philippians 3:14

March 28

Have you ever wondered how long it will be before I come again?

Oh, I wish it were tomorrow! I would love to have the pain and suffering on earth be over. But many things have to happen first.

What I want you to focus on is how real I am in your life right now.

Yes, one day we will be face to face, arm in arm.

For now, our relationship is based on faith; faith that says you know I am with you; faith that says you know I love you, and faith that says you know we will be together forever one day.

Faith can be easy, as easy as a child who just believes and trusts.

Things get murky in this complicated world. Don't focus on the evil here. Find a place of beauty that I created and spend time there talking to Me, recharging your faith.

You need the morning recharge with Me to have the strength to carry you through the day. Take time for these precious moments with Me. It is what you need today, dear one.

Our connection is the strength you need.

*The life I now live in the body, I live by faith in the Son of
God, Who loved me and gave Himself for me.*
Galatians 2:20

March 29

Do you hear the voices of angels? Their songs fill the air with praise. They are My heavenly messengers.

One day your eyes and ears will be uncovered, and you will hear their mighty chorus, and you will join in. Your voice will be a perfectly pitched one with the ability to scale high and low notes perfectly.

You are surrounded everywhere by these angels who help Me minister to My loved ones. They go back and forth from heaven, watching over those who trust in Me.

But now you see through a glass darkly and your relationship with Me is one of faith and not sight. Just trust Me, beloved one. It is all very real. You are loved, cared for and protected by Me and a very large host of angels.

Do not despair. One day you will join in the heavenly host singing joyful songs of praise to Me.

But for now, rest your soul.
I am with you today.

Suddenly a great company of the heavenly host appeared
with the angel, praising God and saying, "Glory to God
in the highest heaven, and on earth peace to those
on whom His favor rests."
Luke 2:13-14

March 30

In the silence of your heart, I send messages of love for you to feel and to share.

Because you have been learning how to listen to Me, I am able to send them to you more and more.

Oh, how empty the world is of love! What I see and know would horrify you. There is evil everywhere. You cannot even imagine what some people do to others every day. Sin has settled over them and they are lost to Me, lost to eternal life.

That's one reason our connection is so important. I need you to stand tall and firm against the dark forces that surround you.

Together we are more powerful than anything.

So, do not be afraid. Every day decisions must be made for good or for evil.

Choose Christ and Him crucified. All sin must flee.

My message of love must, and will, win.

You are My precious, chosen child.

> *Finally, be strong in the Lord and in His mighty power. Put on the full armor of God, so that you can take your stand against the devil's schemes. For our struggle is not against flesh and blood, but against the rulers, against the authorities, against the powers of this dark world and against the spiritual forces of evil in the heavenly realms.*
> *Ephesians 6:10-12*

March 31

I want to tell you something, dear one. My love for you stretches far beyond the boundaries of what you can understand.

It is all you will ever need in your entire life.

You don't need money, possessions or even a close loved one when you learn how to rely on Me.

The loneliness that you feel will melt away the deeper you allow our relationship to grow. I know when you suffer loneliness, and it hurts Me.

I want you to have loved ones in your life, and a special loved one to spend time with. But this may not be the right time.

I want to reach out and hold you to My chest until the suffering stops., but I can only come as close as you let Me.

The peace and love I offer will ease your loneliness and you will enjoy spending more and more time with Me.

Come, sit at My feet, and let Me tell you a story.

It's all about Him. And Me. And you

"Before long, the world will not see Me anymore, but you will see Me. Because I live, you also will live. On that day you will realize that I am in My Father, and you are in Me, and I am in you."
John 14:19-20

April 01

The path to victory is not won through weak-minded people. It is won through My chosen ones.

Chosen and prepared. Chosen and trained.

Every moment danger swirls around you, yet you are safe and strong as long as you keep your eyes on Me.

You are My strong soldier, ready not only to fight the evil one, but to reach out and help others.

So much is happening now, dear one, and I need you to stay strong. Don't let depression or fear weigh you down.

If you lean on Me you are strong. You cannot be strong on your own.

I am your strength, your shield.

Through Me and with Me you can conquer anything I put in front of you.

Chosen and prepared. Chosen and trained.
Chosen to be My child, with Me forever.

The Lord is my strength and my defense; He has become my salvation. He is my God, and I will praise Him, my father's God and I will exalt Him.
Exodus 15:2

April 02

I want to give you My strength.

Yes, I need you to believe that it is possible. In belief there is power. All power is called down from on high. It is around you all the time.

A full commitment to Me is the first start.

A broken soldier kneeling at My feet receives a blanket of power and strength stronger than one hundred or one thousand men.

What do you need so much power for?

The time is coming when I will call you out of your quiet life and ask you, like Abraham and Moses, to be great for Me.

But for now, come and lay your head on My chest and receive the peace and the strength I give My loved and chosen ones.

There is a battle all around you, dear one.

But for now, just be My child, lost in a Father's embrace.

But He said to me, "My grace is sufficient for you, for My power is made perfect in weakness." Therefore I will boast all the more gladly about my weaknesses, so that Christ's power may rest on me.
2 Corinthians 12:9

April 03

There is a hurting world out there, loved one. Even those who look successful and happy are hurting inside. They are frightened when they lay their heads down at night.

Are you doing that? I have spelled out the plan of salvation clearly in the Bible so that you would not be one whose soul cries out in the dark.

Where are you, My child? Do you know? Do you feel it in your soul? Does it fill up all the empty spots with love and warmth?

It is where I long to be: one with you, as Jesus and I are One.

Do you remember His prayer in the book of John asking that you and I may be one as He and I are? His blood was poured out on Calvary so that that very request was made possible.

Your fear, or fright, is only a sign that you have not accepted Me into your life as much as you can.

Come and let us be one, as Jesus and I are. Let My love overflow through every pore in your body.

Soak Me in, dear one.
Find the joy and peace Christ purchased for you many years ago.

"My prayer is not for them alone. I pray also for those who will believe in Me through their message, that all of them may be one, Father, just as You are in Me and I am in You. May they also be in Us so that the world may believe that You have sent Me."
John 17:20-21

April 04

Your soul is crying out to Me now. I see it and I feel it.

It is time for you to go to your quiet place, close your eyes, relax and sense My presence.

As you are resting, imagine a man walking alongside his child. They stop walking because in front of them is a deep and treacherous path.

Now, imagine that father reaching down tenderly and picking his child up in his arms. He carries his child along the path with sure, strong steps.

That child is you, dear one.

I love you so much that I have picked you up in My arms and am carrying you over life's road.

You are not alone, and you are not uncared for. You are so tenderly cared for and loved that when you look back at the path, you will see one set of footprints, much larger than yours.

I will guide you and help you, My child.

Just trust Me.

This is love: not that we loved God, but that He loved us and sent His Son as an atoning sacrifice for our sins
I John 4:10

April 05

*N*ow and forever you have entered into a relationship with Me.

There was a time when you first accepted Me into your life. How Heaven's bells rang that day! We all rejoiced at one of our own coming into the fold!

We knew it would happen and yet when it did, we could not have rejoiced more than if it was a total surprise!

How you are loved and watched over!

We see everything and everyone you encounter, and we watch you with pride. Yet, sometimes you act as if you are always alone and that no one sees, and no one cares! Nothing could be farther from the truth, dear one.

Your life and everything that happens in it is of utmost importance to Us. It has been since the day you were born, and now that you are seeking a closer walk with Me, joy fills Heaven's gate and we are one.

Don't ever let anything separate us, dear one.

You are Mine and I am yours.

The Lord will keep you from all harm – He will watch over
your life; the Lord will watch over your coming and
going both now and forevermore.
Psalm 121:7-8

April 06

Let the joy rise up in your soul this morning and let My love flow over you as you bask in My favor.

You are My cherished child. Imperfect in so many ways, yet because of Christ's death on the cross, the shedding of His blood for you, I see you as My perfect lamb, but one that is hurting and scared inside.

Oh, My dear one, do not be. I watch over you like an eagle watches its prey as he soars in the skies.

I long to swoop down and gather you up unto Myself.

But for right now, you are where you need to be. I am training you to be a strong warrior for Me.

Yes, My little lamb is needed in this world, a very important piece of the puzzle.

Keep listening. Keep trusting.
You are Mine and I am yours.

Have I not commanded you? Be strong and courageous. Do not be afraid; do not be discouraged, for the Lord your God will be with you wherever you go.
Joshua 1:9

April 07

*F*eel My presence, My beloved child. Let the light of My goodness pervade your soul. Breathe in the sanity of My Holy Spirit.

Now, face the day.

You are clothed with My power and light.
Nothing can touch you today.

Share My love with the hurting population around you, those who are frightened by world events happening quickly. Let them know about the bright future you have waiting for you. Let them know I see their suffering and I am the answer through it all.

satan would have this generation believe there is no hope, only pain and suffering. He would have them discount the death and resurrection of My perfect Son as trivial nonsense, and not reality. He would have them believe in Christ's goodness as a person, and the unity of world religions.

He knows the only way to Me is through Christ and he will do anything he can to have this generation turn away from the One Perfect Gift.

Tell them, dear one.

You are holding truth in your hand that will release souls from death into life and happiness. Tell them there is one way to Me and the knowledge of Him will bring joy and love such as they have never felt in their lives.

Jesus answered, "I am the way and the truth and the life. No one comes to the Father except through Me. If you really know Me, you will know My Father as well."
John 14:6-7

April 08

*T*he Truth is a beacon of light to the world.

It is the story of salvation, so beautifully presented in the gospels of the Bible, and handed down through generations.

Since then, there are many more stories of shed blood and mighty conquerors carrying on the message. It has covered the earth through missionaries and brothers and sisters in Christ, My mighty soldiers!

The U.S. was founded on principles of faith but now it is moving step by step to eliminate Me from schools, libraries, court houses, and even from the Constitution itself. One day Americans will know the price it will have to pay to remove Me.

You think of yourself as a simple child, yet I envision you as a mighty warrior carrying My light to those around you.

You are part of a surging, moving tide that is crushing the evil forces that try to rise up against Me.

One day you will know, dear one, all the lives you have touched just by sharing My love in simple ways.

Come and refresh yourself in your quiet place. A whole world awaits My beacon of light, but for now, rest your head on My shoulder.

For you have chosen Me.

I became a servant of this gospel by the gift of God's grace
given me through the working of His power.
Ephesians 3:7

April 09

The picture I gave you several days ago of Me carrying you was My gift to you so that you will know, now and always, how I love and care for you.

You may think the world is falling down around you, but I am right beside you, loving and caring for you.

Remember your "thus far" rock? The rock you found and put in your house so you could look at it whenever you were frightened and worried that the world was going to come crashing down around you? The rock is a reminder that "thus far" I have carried you.

You are still standing, and "thus far" I will continue carrying you.

I will never let you down nor will I will ever let you go.

The vision of Me carrying you when you think you can go no farther should always be able to be called to mind.

And when you feel so alone, know that You are not, for I have picked you up and we are walking through the storm together.

So do not fear, for I am with you; do not be dismayed, for I am your God. I will strengthen you and help you; I will uphold you with My righteous right hand.
Isaiah 41:10

April 10

Can you hear the birds sing their notes of praise to Me this morning? How loudly they proclaim their joy and thanks!

In the midst of all your problems and the cares of the world, do you take time to thank Me? To praise Me?

Fix your eyes on Me, dear one, the Author and Finisher of your faith. Things that seemed so dark and murky will become clear to you.

Don't see things as the world sees them. See them for what they are.

My little warrior! How proud I am of you!

When you return to your quiet place and say, "I choose You, Lord," as you kneel before Me, I cover you with My loving arms and seek to fill your soul with peace.

My little soldier is home again, safely in My arms!

The Mighty One, God, the Lord, speaks and summons the
earth from the rising of the sun to where it sets.
And the heavens proclaim His righteousness,
for He is a God of justice.
Psalm 50:1, 6

April 11

When you left your home to face the world, whether it was to go to work, or go grocery shopping, or to play a game of soccer, whatever it was, you left the safety of your quiet place.

You could not see what was happening around you, but forces of evil were everywhere.

Were you kind to those around you in the face of impatience or even rudeness? Did you smile at a downcast person, or encourage a friend or loved one? You were doing My work, dear one. And no matter what the devil put in front of you, you stood tall and strong for the principles of love.

So, come now and let Me surround you with My peace.

Someday I will call you to lead in a stronger manner, but for now, I am welcoming My warrior home to renew your strength so that you may rise up on the wings of an eagle.

Even youths grow tired and weary, and young men stumble
and fall; but those who hope in the Lord will renew their
strength. They will soar on wings like eagles; they will run
and not grow weary, they will walk and not be faint.
Isaiah 40:30-31

April 12

Do you think often of the day when there will be no more sickness, no more pain and no more suffering? I, too, long for that day when I can bring all My children home to My care.

A world of joy and peace where only love reigns.

Your body will be strong and beautiful. People will laugh, and if they cry, they will only cry tears of happiness. Loved ones who have gone before will be reunited. There will be no misunderstanding or separations without satan and his discontent.

Only love and joy will be known.

And I will get to walk with you in full vision. You will sit with Me and I will tell you the stories of long ago. There will be many there, but it will seem like you and I are alone together.

No more pain, dear one.
Hang on to that promise, for it is real. Very real.

For I so loved the world that I gave My only begotten Son that whosoever should believe in Me should not perish but should come and live in Heaven, forever with Me.

For God so loved the world that He gave His one and only Son, that whoever believes in Him shall not perish but have eternal life. For God did not send his Son into the world to condemn the world, but to save the world through Him.
John 3:16-17

April 13

Are you My soldier? Do you feel like you are alone in a coliseum with a maddening crowd jeering at you, taunting you?

If you could only see the throngs of angels that would surround you if you bent your knee and asked Me for cover!

My child is never alone.

I know you feel that way often. Fight back. Don't let it overcome you.

Reach out for My presence.

Spend time in prayer with Me, talking to Me. Tell Me your fears, your problems. Bring Me your pain and your loneliness.

I will surround you with love and a feeling of warmth. My child will never stand alone in a coliseum or anywhere on earth. The battle was WON at the cross so that you and I may be one as Jesus and I are one.

Rise up with joy and courage. Face this day and all its challenges with My promise of My continued presence in you and with you.

Now and forever.

I keep my eyes always on the Lord. With Him at my right hand, I will not be shaken. You make known to me the path of life; You will fill me with joy in Your presence, with eternal pleasures at Your right hand.
Psalm 16:8, 11

April 14

*O*h, the joy of a new day! There is so much that I want you to cherish and enjoy!

First, take out the trash. By trash, I mean the garbage inside your mind. Clear all your problems, hang-ups, unforgiveness, and insecurities out of your mind.

Lay them at My feet. I will toss them out for you. And don't try to grab them and hold onto them as they pass you by!

You don't have the strength on your own to do this "house cleaning". Only I can do it for you.

Now you are a clean slate for Me to mold and develop to be the person I created you to be.

Open your Bible and read the Psalms. See where David learned of Me and praised Me. He, like you, was FAR from perfect, yet he always took time out to praise and worship Me. We were close, and I was able to rule a nation through him.

What are My plans to do with this new, cleaned up you? Just wait and see.

Trust Me.
I have much in store for you this day!

> *But I, by your great love, can come into Your house;*
> *in reverence I bow down toward Your holy temple.*
> *Lead me, Lord, in Your righteousness because of*
> *my enemies make Your way straight before me.*
> *Psalm 5:7-8.*

April 15

Let not your heart be troubled. You believe in Me. You believe in My Son. You believe in the Holy Spirit.

In Heaven there is a mansion which I have prepared for you. Do you have a mansion here, or is it a simple home? It makes no difference, for I have already prepared a lovely home just for you.

A home where you can freely come and go. One where you can invite guests over to share stories of love and praise. A home where health and happiness reigns. A home you will leave in the morning to do the work I have prepared for you to do, work which you love because it involves all the talents and desires I have given you.

When you return in the evening, you will feel lighthearted and happy.

Six days you will work and on the seventh you will join all of heaven as we gather together and rejoice finally that sin, pain, evil and sorrow is gone forever and ever and only joy and peace and love remain.

Your voices will rise in joyous union praising Me. How blest that day will be! All My beloved ones will be together at last!! I can hardly wait, dear one!

Live life as if this day is just around the corner. Live life preparing for your big house on the hill: the house of love, laughter and praise that I have built for you already, that where I am, there you may be also!

"And if I go and prepare a place for you, I will come back
and take you to be with Me that you
also may be where I am."
John 14:3

April 16

It is a hungry world out there, beloved. A hungry world that cannot be satisfied with the things on this earth; a people who long for happiness and love but who cannot find it.

Some are openly unhappy, and others seem like they have the perfect life. But without Me they are empty and scared inside with the reality of their existence getting louder and more visible every day.

You have the answer, dear one. You hold in your hand the key to true happiness, here, now and forevermore.

Are you going to keep that secret just between us, or are you going to let it out?

Like a beautiful butterfly hatching from its cocoon, the whole world will take on new meaning as you share the glorious news with those I have carefully positioned around you.

Let them see the new day, too, My beloved child.

Only in Me is there true happiness and everlasting life.

How, then, can they call on the One they have not believed in? And how can they believe in the One of whom they have not heard? And how can they hear without someone preaching to them? And how can anyone preach unless they are sent? As it is written: "How beautiful are the feet of those who bring good news!"
Romans 10:14-15

April 17

Come to Me this morning, My love. Come into My presence and let Me enter your heart. Let Me show you things that you have not seen before, things which will gladden your soul.

I was with you before you were born. I saw you in your mother's womb. I wove you together with My fingers, and when you were born, I rejoiced at the tiny wisps of your hair, the shape of your body, your fingers and toes . . . and I was pleased.

You have been through so much in your life, yet I have always been with you. Just as I formed your body in love, I stood beside you in your pain and fear. I have also stood beside you in times of happiness. How My heart quickened at the joy you felt, and how heavy it was when you were in pain!

You didn't know that there were times that I picked you up and carried you Myself, and when you awoke, you didn't know that I was right beside you . . . always.

To understand that kind of love more completely, open the Bible and read about how I gave My Son to die for you, so that one day we may see each other face to face and you will know, you will see, and you will feel My arms around you.

You can't comprehend that kind of love yet on this earth. But close your eyes and listen to My Spirit and sense it . . . for I have put it in your soul.

> *My frame was not hidden from You when I was made in the*
> *secret place, when I was woven together in the depths of the*
> *earth Your eyes saw my unformed body . . .*
> *when I awake, I am still with You.*
> *Psalm 139:15-16, 18*

April 18

Today is the beginning of a new day, the start of a life of joy in your heart. You have always had joy, but this is a new joy,

the joy of knowing Me in a very real and personal way.

The closer you get to Me the more your life will make sense.

The more time you spend with Me, the more you will want to because I will unfold before you the beauty of My presence. I will open the door of wondering into a new horizon of love and trust, a bright sunshine far better than the gloom you have been in.

Come and walk there with Me now. Let Me lead you to the light of My countenance. Let people around you see Who your God is! Wear Me like a shield of love.

Yes, I am here with you, beloved one.

Come and experience the joy of truly knowing Me.

You make known to me the path of life; You will fill me
with joy in Your presence, with eternal
pleasures at Your right hand.
Psalm 16:11

April 19

Do you hear the songs of angels? They are all around you, ministering spirits sent to care for My beloved ones.

There is a whole world just outside your senses. Evil is being played out against good. The world you see is filled with pain and suffering.

What you can't see are the angels helping those who cry out, who are in tears themselves at the horrors they see.

The devil is running amok, desperately trying to get as many people as he can to join his side before his rule here ends. You see his anger and frustration played out as thousands are lost in disasters.

What you can't see are My ministering angels covering those people with love as their souls are put to rest. And yet there is so much joy around, too.

The joy of a newborn coming into the world, joy of a newfound love, of a recovered illness and many, many more joys so numerous to mention it would take a book.

It is easy to see what is of Me and what is of the evil one. Stay close, dear one. Don't ever let him get between us.

Stay in My protection and care.

Just know the angels are all around you singing songs of praise to Me.

For He will command His angels concerning you
to guard you in all your ways;
Psalm 91:11

April 20

Are you in great despair, beloved one? Do you feel like there is no answer for what you are going through? That there is no way out, no future? Oh, My love, there is.

I created you, and when I did, I made a plan for your life. There is no need to despair. These feelings you have are temporary. This, too, will pass. You must believe that. You will rise again with joy in the morning.

Never give up. I will guide you through this. Your pain seems unbearable at times. Reach out your hand and let Me take it in Mine. Mine is warm and loving.

There is no pain that together we cannot overcome, no horror in your past that together we cannot pass through. Take one step at a time towards the light I've prepared for you here. You may never know true love and acceptance on this earth, but you know Me and I know you.

There is no greater love on earth than what I have for you. I gave My Son to die for you. No greater love can ever be shown.

What you can't see, I ask you to feel. Feel the comfort of My presence and My continual guidance in your life. Let Me hold you in My arms until your pain stops.

Never give up fighting for the breakthrough of joy. Never give up on Me, for I WILL NEVER GIVE UP ON YOU, and on trying to show you My love.

Fixing our eyes on Jesus, the pioneer and perfecter of faith. For the joy set before Him He endured the cross, scorning its shame, and sat down at the right hand of the throne of God.
Hebrews 12:2

April 21

You are My chosen child, so precious in My sight .

I have gone to Heaven to prepare a place for you to come and be with Me forever.

But now you are feeling alone, dear one. You are not now, or ever, alone.

I am always with you.

Are you afraid? Do not be afraid of anything. Everything you are facing I knew about before time began. And I have armed you with the strength and ability to not only face it, but to conquer it beautifully.

I have trained you for this moment, for this adventure.

You are well armed with Me and a host of angels at your side. Try to envision us walking with you everywhere you go. Only, don't worry about holding the door open for us. We don't face those challenges!

Be assured that the child of the King will never walk in alone!

You are a conqueror because you chose Me,
and because you choose Me every day!

*The Lord is my light and my salvation - whom shall I
fear? The Lord is the stronghold of my life - of
whom shall I be afraid?*
Psalm 27:1

April 22

The feeling you had the other day of Me holding you was real, dear one.

It was something I have been wanting to share with you for a long time. Someday you will be in that embrace.

You will see Me. You will feel My arms around you.
You will know the absolute security in Me.

But for now, close your eyes and envision it. Know, dear one, know, that I am with you.

Lay your head on My shoulder and let Me fill you with My love and strength and power; the power of the Holy Spirit that will be in you to guide and direct your ways and your words.

When you come away from our time together you will be able to face whatever is before you today.

One day at a time. One step at a time.

Close your eyes, dear one, and come to rest at My side.

My loving arms await.

According to His eternal purpose that He accomplished in Christ Jesus our Lord. In Him and through faith in Him we may approach God with freedom and confidence.
Ephesians 3:11-12

April 23

*Y*ou are reaching out to Me this morning.

Your desire is to get to know Me and to be closer to Me. How pleased I am! My heart is full of joy that My beloved one wants a closer walk with Me.

Just put one foot in front of the other today. Don't just read these words but open your Bible and let Me speak to you through it. You will be warmed and comforted by reading the words.

Do this today, putting one foot in front of the other, conquering the fear and loneliness that surround you.

Do not let yourself fall into the chasm of loneliness. There are people all around you. Reach out for them. Right now you may only think it is you and Me. But you and Me mean many others that need to be reached with the good news of My love.

Reach out for My hand.
I have so much in store for you!
Come and pour your heart out before Me now.

*For everything that was written in the past was written to
teach us, so that through the endurance taught in
the Scriptures and the encouragement they
provide we might have hope.*
Romans 15:4

April 24

Why are you so scared of the future? You feel so alone, yet you are not alone, for I am with you. You can sense My presence now if you would take the time to come and pour out your heart to Me.

I am so close to you right now. If you are in a hospital bed, or beside someone there, or you are alone in your house, or if you even feel alone in a group of people, I am here to tell you today, that you are NOT alone.

Sometimes you ache so badly from it that you can hardly breathe. How I want to come and scoop you up into My arms and comfort you!

Oh, My love, come away with Me! Close your eyes and envision My presence, sitting or walking right beside you, for I am right now, My love. I AM, and I always will be.

I will never leave you or forsake you. You are the child I gave so much up for. No matter how old you are, you will be forever My child.

Reach your hands up now and put them around My neck. Let Me draw you into My loving care. The peace will flow through your entire body.

Now you must imagine and believe, but not forever. One day, My precious child, you will see the world through joy. I will watch you run and skip through glorious flowers of red and yellow, in a land where only love reigns.

Until that time, you will never be alone.
Never.

My flesh and my heart may fail, but God is the strength
of my heart and my portion forever.
Psalm 73:26

April 25

*Y*ou may fall, dear one, but you are never out of My care and love.

Don't allow the devil to make you feel separated from Me because you strayed away for a moment, or even downright sinned. His whole goal is to separate us.

Just come back to Me by coming to your quiet place and rest in My presence until you sense the security of My peace inside you.

You can have that, dear one. Christ prayed that we might be one as He and I are One.

His death made that possible.

So never think for a moment that any sin can separate us. Come and cleanse yourself in Me by asking forgiveness and then start anew, washed by the blood of the Lamb of God.

Come now and regain, or start for the first time, the precious relationship with Me that will satisfy you, filling the longing in your soul like no other.

I am here now and forever.
Always loving, always waiting.

Therefore, there is now no condemnation for those who are
in Christ Jesus, because through Christ Jesus the law
of the Spirit Who gives life has set you free
from the law of sin and death.
Romans 8:1-2

April 26

*Y*our heart is breaking today, and you can't see the love I wish to consume you with. Can't I make the pain go away?

Let this time of pain be one where you and I draw closer together, where your feelings for Me, your need of Me, runs long and deep, filling up a chasm of darkness with love. Let Me comfort you through the emptiness and fear you are experiencing.

How much do I love you? Oh, My dear, it cannot be measured or explained in your words, or in any words. We are on a never-ending trip together to discover that love.

You are in My love. You were created out of love. You were created for love, for Me, Who IS love.

Lie down and let Me float you through quiet waters of love and peace. You are here with Me now. Relax, close your eyes and let Me guide you. The water is rocking you gently on each side, but you are in peace, and love.

You are not feeling the fear or pain now, just peace in knowing that you are loved so much. I will not let you sink. Rest completely in My arms and you will float more freely.

For right now, that is how to say I love you. You will feel it when you learn to trust Me and to relax in My arms.

I AM LOVE.

Trust in the Lord forever, for the Lord, the Lord
Himself, is the Rock eternal.
Isaiah 26:4

April 27

You desire a closer union with Me. I want to grant you that union.

To be one with Me in your heart and soul will be truly wonderful. You may strive all you want for this union but the true beauty in your heart and soul is a gift from Me. It can never be attained on your own.

There are those who have spent their lives doing good works trying to attain not only this "goodness" but eternal life, as well. My heart goes out to reach them constantly, asking them to receive the Holy Spirit, to receive Jesus Christ into their lives, and if they accept these gifts, eternal life, as well.

But many just go on their way in their effort to attain perfection through works. I am not in their souls. I am not in their hearts. This is a form of evil itself. The devil will even use good works to keep their eyes off Me.

Do not give up trying to help these souls, as their hearts are crying out for Me. They hope by doing good works they will fill the emptiness in their souls, but it will only be found in Me. Receipt of My gift will set them free to love and laugh and to reach out to others for the right reasons.

Come close and commune with Me. Embrace the gift of My Son Jesus Christ.

You and Me. Me and You.

So we, too, have put our faith in Christ Jesus that we may be justified by faith in Christ and not by the works of the law, because by the works of the law no one will be justified.
Galatians 2:16

April 28

My child is forever young to Me, forever free and wild. I see you running down a hill with the wind in your hair, freely taking in exuberant joy.

Is that vision of your life here on earth? No. And in fact, you may not even be able to imagine it. There is loss, hardship and pain all around you but freedom and unabandoned joy is your future.

For now, stay in My presence. Draw near to Me.
I am your strength. I am your guide. With Me all things will become clear.

You don't understand the pain you or others must go through. And sometimes you cry out wondering where I am.

I am with you, My love.

Through the hardest of times, I have never left your side. You are still here, standing, in communion with Me.

Remember your "thus far" rock, the rock I asked you to find and keep close to you so that when you look at it, it would be a remembrance that I have brought you this far, and that you are still standing and that I will never leave you.

Hold on to that knowledge and don't let go, because I will never let you go.

Even to your old age and gray hairs I am He, I am He who will sustain you. I have made you and I will carry you; I will sustain you and I will rescue you.
Isaiah 46:4

April 29

Look at the beauty of nature all around you. It is the closest revelation of Me.

Do you live in a concrete jungle with little visible sign of Me? Take time to travel to the beauty of a hillside or park where lush grass grows and tiny flowers bud, where birds sing, and squirrels run happily to and fro.

I created these things.

Spend time there and appreciate the wonder of creation as you study the trees and flowers. You will feel My presence close to you, a slight wind like My breath on your skin.

If it is not possible to spend time in nature, close your eyes and call out My name, for My promise that I will never leave you, no matter where you are, is very real.

While easier to sense Me in the glory of My creation, I will draw near to you no matter where you are.

Just call out My name.

For since the creation of the world God's invisible qualities -
His eternal power and divine nature - have been clearly
seen, being understood from what has been made,
so that people are without excuse.
Romans 1:20

April 30

The wind is blowing through the trees, bringing with it a change in the weather.

Are you ready for the change? Come and let Me show you the way. The way will not be an easy one but one in which I will never leave you.

There will be times when you feel like you must give up. But fear not, for I am with you and am guiding you through the stormy seas.

There is light and peace at the other end.

Do not despair. Others will fall by the wayside as they make the choice for ease and comfort. But you are following the plan I have for you. It will become clearer every day because I have given you the Holy Spirit to guide and direct you, baptizing you with Him when you came to know Me.

By staying in tune with Him you will not be led astray.

Learn to listen. His words are like the wind blowing outside, so clear to those who are ready and so unclear to those who are not willing to listen and obey.

Listen to the gentle wind in your soul. It is the true direction.

Dear friends, do not be surprised at the fiery ordeal that has come on you to test you, as though something strange were happening to you. But rejoice inasmuch as you participate in the sufferings of Christ, so that you may be overjoyed when His glory is revealed.
I Peter 4:12-13

May 01

Your soul is stilled. You receive peace. There is quietness in your soul.

The peace and joy I give you can never be compared to any other thing. A peace in your soul that knows, really knows, where you came from, and knows, really knows, where you are going.

The stuff of daily life in the middle is where you experience the pain and sorrow that each of you must bear.

Keep your focus on Me and experience total calmness in your soul in the midst of the world.

This world is not your home. I am your home. Only through Me can true joy be attained.

Unbelievers cannot understand. Only when they are ready and I send them the Holy Spirit, will they begin to think about it.

Every step taken with Me is a foundation for the next one. Just take one small step at a time. I will not ask you to take overwhelming strides.

You will have peace in your soul through the best of times and through the worst of times because . . .

you have chosen Me, and I have chosen you.

He rescues me unharmed from the battle waged against
me, even though many oppose me.
Psalm 55:18

May 02

*A*mazing grace, how sweet the sound!!

The words in that hymn are very powerful. They say so much about the plan of salvation, something that can never be earned. It makes Christ's death on the cross even stronger because you begin to understand how much of a gift it was.

There were not many people on earth at that time who were sorry to see Him die. He did not step into death to save the life of someone else who was to die that day. No, Jesus gave Himself to die for those who flogged Him.

And I, I allowed it to happen.

Sorrow and darkness that you can never comprehend filled Heaven. I had to turn away as My Son took his last breath. When it was over, I tore the curtain in the sanctuary, forever signifying that His death was not in vain.

His death was life! And light! And love far greater than any other.

Come now and let it fill your soul. A gift, available to all who would accept His sacrifice, who would say,

"I choose You, Lord Jesus! I choose You!"

Amazing grace, how sweet the sound! How precious, how true.

For all have sinned and fall short of the glory of God,
and all are justified freely by His grace through the
redemption that came by Christ Jesus.
Romans 3:23-24

May 03

There is a peace to the morning as the stillness slowly begins to fade. Birds start singing their praises in the meadow, calling out to each other with their individual notes.

As you start to stir, I watch as you arise from your bed. Do you awake with fear, or do you confidently say, "I choose You!"? This short daily affirmation goes a long way in keeping sin and temptation away and enabling Me to draw closer to you.

"I choose You!" Those words ring into My very soul and I cover My child with My shield of protection.

It is a good morning! Rise and take My hand of strength! Let Me make you aware of the beauty unfolding just right within your hearing, the wonder of creation coming alive! Let your soul rise in the awakening as you seek My presence today.

So much to look forward to, so much we can do together today! Rise tall and stand transfixed as I fill every inch of you with love, goodness, courage and honor.

You are My special, chosen child and our time together in the morning, surrounded by the awakening of the world around you, will instill peace and courage in your soul.

Choose Me, for I have chosen you.

You will go out in joy and be led forth in peace; the
mountains and hills will burst into song before you,
and all the trees of the field will clap their hands.
Isaiah 55:12

May 04

Oh, dear child, I am pleased that you are seeking My presence, and that you have dedicated yourself to righteousness.

The books in heaven are filled with many people who have given themselves to Me. And each one of them is very different. I created a special plan for them, yet the final picture would not be fulfilled without you. It would be like looking at a beautiful painting with a hole in it if you did not fulfill your mission.

Your life and actions will touch many people you are not aware of, just by the simple way you reach out to others. It is like a snowball effect: the goodness rolling and growing larger and larger.

Don't let that frighten or intimidate you. You are so precious to Me. I knew what you could do from before the time you were born into this world.

And I put in you a desire to do it, blessing you with the special talents needed in order to accomplish this mission.

And I have never left your side, encouraging you every step of the way.

Come now, reach up for My hand and guidance, and let Me lead you on our journey, together.

You are My beloved child in whom I am pleased.

The Lord your God is with you, the Mighty Warrior who saves. He will take great delight in you; in His love He will no longer rebuke you, but will rejoice over you with singing.
Zephaniah 3:17

May 05

*D*ay after day you wonder when all the hardship will end. Yet why do some of My other followers laugh? Why do some seem to have no pain and fear when you are strapped with heavy burdens? You want to be like them.

Don't look to others, dear one. Look to Me. Look into My eyes.

I have set you apart for Me. I have put you on this road for a reason. Through the testing and the fire, you will be refined as fine gold, ready to accomplish My purpose for your life.

I will give you strength to carry on that you don't know you have; strength to face seemingly impossible situations with a peace in your soul that can only be shared with Me.

It is our private peace. It can be talked about with others, but this is something you cannot give away. It is My gift to you, our sacred connection.

Strive for that and everything else will become clear. Your problems will fall away at the side of the road and light will mark the end of the tunnel.

So do not envy those who love Me and seem to have it all. Let Me worry about them. Keep your eyes on Me.

This is about you and Me, and Me and you.
Now and forever.

"Don't be afraid, Daniel. Since the first day that you set your mind to gain understanding and to humble yourself before your God, your words were heard, and I have come in response to them."
Daniel 10:12

May 06

Let joy pervade every cell of your body! Let laughter ring out in your soul! You are My chosen child and there is so much to be thankful for!

You have presented your problems to Me. Now drop them in My hand and let Me deal with them. Concentrate on loving those around you, getting to know Me through My Word and through the beauties of nature. Let this day be one of renewal into the glorious body of Christ.

Where are you, child? Are you with Me?

Take My hand and let Me lead you up the path I have chosen for you. All your cares are in My hand, and your job is to seek Me with all your heart, mind and soul.

And laugh. Laugh from the very recesses of your soul. Laughter is the spilling out, the overflowing of the joy inside your being. Let Me watch My beloved sing and dance with joy and laughter.

What joy? What laughter? In the eternal life I have given you through My Son Jesus whose death on the cross insured your ability to live with Me forever!

You have made that choice. Now, revel in its beauty, in its joy, in its lightness of being.

And laugh, My love. Laugh.
It is good.

> *Though you have not seen Him, you love Him; and even*
> *though you do not see Him now, you believe in Him and*
> *are filled with an inexpressible and glorious joy.*
> *I Peter 1:8*

May 07

True humility is true beauty.

A humble heart is like medicine to your soul. Those who rush around importantly have no real connection to Me because the connection comes from the heart of love and brokenness poured out to Me.

Then I will come and comfort them, and they shall know Me and know My ways.

Do not let the worries of this world overwhelm you. They are there to bring you to Me.

True humility is not just an attribute, it emanates from the depth of your soul. It comes when you truly understand the plan of salvation and the extreme love We had for you to allow Christ to die on the cross when you were still a sinner.

True humility towards Us, yet a quiet pride that you are the child of the King of the universe, that you were found worthy, not by your goodness or works, but because you were covered by the blood of Christ, to come into a family of believers, and not as a newcomer, but as one who was chosen and planned for since the beginning of time.

Humility for this incredible gift to an unworthy recipient.

And just plain outrageous joy at being part of the family!!

Therefore, as God's chosen people, holy and dearly loved,
clothe yourselves with compassion, kindness,
humility, gentleness and patience.
Colossians 3:12

May 08

"Remain in Me, and I will remain in you", a promise given long ago by Jesus, and just as true today. If you remain in Me, and I in you, you may ask whatever you wish, and I will grant it.

You see, if you stay connected to Me, your requests will be in My will. The things you ask will glorify Me.

I will always answer. The result may not be the one you are looking for, but it is the one I know is best for you. That is where trust comes from.

Know that I will answer in the way that is best for you, for others and for the situation. And then rise up with a light heart, cast the cares off of your shoulders and go about your day trusting that I will take care of it in My time.

Remain in Me throughout the day, listening to My urgings, wondering at creation, reading the Word, praising Me with songs of love.

Oh, how I love you, child! I will draw closer and closer each day that you open the door by remaining in Me.

Soon we will be together forever, face to face. But for now, by faith and by the memory of our time together,

Remain in Me and I will remain in you.

"If you remain in Me and My words remain in you, ask
whatever you wish, and it will be done for you. This is
to My Father's glory, that you bear much fruit,
showing yourselves to be My disciples."
John 15:7-8

May 09

*W*herever you are, I am there.

If you are in the midst of enemy warfare, I am beside you. If you are in the depths of despair, I am there. If your pain is so intense you cry for mercy, and for Me, I am there.

Now, always and forever.

If you are sitting in a busy meeting, or walking outside on a nature trail, I am beside you. Your greatest fear is the lonely life of an outsider. You are never outside, My love. You are on the inside of Me with your love and your heart.

I am in you and you are in Me, a part of Me.

You have My heart.

If it were possible for your earthly father to be with you, he could never gain the access I have, in you, around you, and shining through you to others, for you are Mine.

I am so proud of you and what you have become, and what you WILL become.

> *"And I Myself will be a wall of fire around it," declares*
> *the Lord, "and I will be its glory within."*
> *Zechariah 2:5*

May 10

Difficult times like these require a tough stance. I created you to be a strong soldier for Me in the face of whatever the world throws at you.

You do not stand alone, for a host of armies stand beside you, behind you and in front of you as you face the increasingly unsettled world.

Never be frightened, for no one can take real life away from you. If you have chosen Me, and accepted Christ's death on the cross, you may receive eternal life.

Real life. Your forever life.

When you consider your future with Me, what on this earth could ever make you afraid? Death? No, for that leads to eternal life.

The situations you come up against here are challenging but if you could only see the host of armies that minister to you and come to your aid instantly in response to your prayers to Me, you would not fear.

Remember that I will make ALL things work out together for good to those who love Me. So, stand strong, My soldier!! You are Mine and I am yours. Together we can face and overcome any challenge!

In all these things we are more than conquerors through Him who loved us. For I am convinced that neither death nor life, neither angels nor demons, neither the present nor the future, nor any powers, neither height nor depth, nor anything else in all creation, will be able to separate us from the love of God that is in Christ Jesus our Lord.
Romans 8:37-39

May 11

I want to be with you forever.

But the real forever is a concept you cannot yet comprehend. For as long as eternity, I wish to see you, be with you, walk with you, and to speak with you.

My love for you will never diminish.

Come and take My hand. Walk with me through the portals of time and space and just spend time with Me. My heart yearns for it, for you are the beloved child who I created for Me.

I placed every eyelash over your eyes. I made you a heart to beat with life and love. I gave you strong legs to walk on to bear My gospel message and I gave you a soul to seek after Me.

Are you listening to your soul? For I am calling.
Can you hear the whisperings of My heart towards you?

Ever since you were young, I have guided and protected you, waiting to draw you into a deeper relationship with Me. That time is here and now, My child. Take this moment to reach out and take My hand, saying "I choose You!".

Remain in Me and I in you.
Find your joy, our joy.
True joy.

> *The Lord is the everlasting God, the Creator of the ends of*
> *the earth. He will not grow tired or weary, and His*
> *understanding no one can fathom. He gives strength*
> *to the weary and increases the power of the weak.*
> *Isaiah 40:28-29*

May 12

I will not let you forget, dear one, that I am holding you in My arms.

Through all the problems in this world, through all the pain and sadness you bear, if you look to Me, I will not let you forget that My arms are wrapped tightly around you, seeking to hold and comfort you.

Yea, though you walk through the valley of the shadow of death, you will fear no evil for I am with you, now and forever.

A new world is about to start for you.

Your time of sorrow and despair is coming to an end and I have a bright new world before you.

Just hold My hand and let the adventure continue.

Surely life with Me is the greatest adventure of all, one in which you know the ending. One in which you know that you know that you know! One in which you know there will be a happy, happy ending.

"And My child lived happily ever after."

Even though I walk through the darkest valley, I will fear
no evil, for You are with me; Your rod and
Your staff, they comfort me.
Psalm 23:4

May 13

Are you excited about the new life you are facing? Do not be afraid.

Walk into the unknown with Me at your side. You will be forever blessed.

Do you seek wisdom for this future? I have promised it, if only you ask.

Do you seek security for this future? The security I have promised is an everlasting one, Heavenly security that I have promised to those who love Me. Earthly security would do you no good right now.

I need you to lean on Me, to depend on Me for every breath of your life.

Seek Me.

Seek wisdom and purity. I am found in the still small voice in your soul. It is the stuff legends are made of, yet you have it available to you at the tip of your fingers.

Take Me and all I offer, to guide and protect you into this new life you are about to start.

Let it be a new life about Me. You will never go wrong!

For the Lord gives wisdom; from His mouth
come knowledge and understanding.
Proverbs 2:6

May 14

𝒪h, My beloved child, so much is in front of you now! You are feeling that you don't have the strength or the power to continue. And you don't understand why I have put you in this position, in this time of need, when all you want to do is serve Me.

Every day I reach out for you, to touch and hold you. Every day you get up and go about your day, stopping to talk to Me when you make the time. It is not about time. It is about eternity and power and strength . . . and about Me.

You think of this world's problems as your own, but they are not. I share every one of them with you. I feel your pain and your disappointment, sometimes leveled at Me. And yet I am in just as much pain over it as well.

When you run out the door in the morning without stopping and spending our precious time together you leave the power and strength behind. How can you conquer these issues without Me? You try, and you try again. Yet it still there, and sometimes you blame Me.

Connect with Me, dear one. Connect with Me. Find joy such as you have never known. You will find that you will be more in tune with Me, learning to trust the outcome of a situation no matter what.

There is peace and joy in Me, only in Me. I will always be waiting, no matter what. Don't ever be afraid to come running back into My arms.

I am waiting now.

I wait for the Lord, my whole being waits,
and in His Word I put my hope.
Psalm 130:5

May 15

You are hurting inside, dear one. Although you try to hide it, I sense it. Not many others know about how you feel, but the One Who loves you does.

I know when you get frightened in the middle of the night, when you feel all alone in the middle of a crowd. I know when you face what seems to be unconquerable odds, either with your health, or your finances, or a personal relationship that is very important to you.

You carry so much of the burden in your being. Come and lay it at My altar. My altar is covered with complete perfect love, forgiveness, and strength. You have access to it at any time. What once seemed impossible is now possible with Me at your side.

I am asking you to open up your heart and your soul to receive My presence.

This healing touch is vital to your overall health and happiness. Only by truly laying your pain and burdens down can you experience true peace.

Search your heart today.

Search me, God, and know my heart; test me and know my
anxious thoughts. See if there is any offensive way in
me and lead me in the way everlasting.
Psalm 139:23-24

May 16

Follow Me up to the stars. Follow Me up to the moon. Reach as far into your dreams as you can to envision a life lived fully with Me. A life of joy without pain. A life of peace without war. A life of love without hate.

Is it there? Is it possible?

Yes, My beloved, it is. One day we will walk hand in hand together in perfect peace and contentment. One day we will look upon the stars and count their numbers. One day mankind will face each other with love and compliance.

But for now, conquer your fears with faith in Me. Faith in the knowledge that there will be a world of love and light, that there will be joy again.

Toss your cares to the ground, laugh in the midst of your sorrow. There will be joy, true, forever JOY!

Where does it come from? How can you really know? Reach into your heart, for I have put that knowledge there. I formed you from the dust of the earth. I made you to see Me when you see My created things: the birds, the mountains, the valleys, the oceans.

You know, dear one. You really, really know.

Just reach into your heart and believe. I am there. Now and always. Never farther away than a thought or a prayer.

By faith we understand that the universe was formed at God's
command, so that what is seen was not made
out of what was visible.
Hebrews 11:3

May 17

You do not have to be a worldly-wise man to be a strong soldier for Me, to lead in the fight of good against evil. You just need a simple relationship with Me.

I need you to have faith like a child, trusting Me at every turn even though you don't understand much of the time why you have to be going through what you are.

Come to Me with faith. With trust.

There are those who lash out in anger towards Me when difficulties arise. If they could only know how much it hurts Me when that happens! Don't they know I will be with them? That all things will work out together for good?

Or they might be angry at Me that their loved one died. I cried with them when they hurt, when they grieved. I cried because of their pain yet they were angry at Me because I allowed it to happen.

It is My desire that all should live everlasting lives filled with joy and peace. And one day that will be the case. But for now, while the saga in this evil world plays out, learn to place your childlike faith in Me. Lay back in the water and float with your eyes closed, knowing, feeling, sensing, that I am with you, in you, all around you. And you are with Me.

Faith like a child is the greatest wisdom in the world.

But Jesus said, "Let the little children come to Me, and
do not hinder them; for the kingdom of Heaven
belongs to such as these."
Matthew 19:14

May 18

Where do you start? You start with Me. Everything starts with Me.

From the beginning of creation and before, I am, I was, and I will continue to be, forever.

And I never waiver. I was the same then as I am now.

I am love so intense you cannot behold My real presence. What I am presenting to you is but a shadow of Who I am.

I am the north, the south, the east, the west. There is nowhere you can go that I will not be found.

Your world is finite, and it is hard to understand that concept, but one day you will see all and understand all. When you see Me face to face you will feel love so intense your whole body will be transformed into light.

So where do you start?
With Me. Now and always.

I am your Forever.

Just take one step towards Me. Just a baby step of faith. I will do the rest.

Deep calls to deep in the roar of your waterfalls; all your waves and breakers have swept over me. By day the Lord directs His love, at night His song is with me, a prayer to the God of my life.
Psalm 42:7-8

May 19

There are times when I sense you doubting My existence, even when I have poured so much love into you.

When bad things happen in the world, or you don't understand the personal pain you are going through, you wonder if I am really real.

I AM real, My love. There is nothing more real.

The drop of dew on your cheek. Is it real? The rumbling of thunder, is it real? These are things that are part of your world, yet you can't hold them in your hands. I am like that.

I live and move in another sense, one in which you can be more aware of the more you spend time with Me. When you are in My presence, I can reveal who I am. I can imbue you with My attributes.

There is a world of pain out there that I am deep in the midst of. Come to Me with your pain, beloved one. Let Me show you My existence. Let Me wrap My arms around you and hold you until the pain is gone, until you are strong enough to stand on your own again.

One day you will know why, My love. One day. Until that time, come into My presence by spending time with Me.

I will come as close as you let Me. Now and forever.

Blessed are those who have learned to acclaim You, who walk in the light of Your presence, Lord. They rejoice in Your name all day long; they celebrate Your righteousness.
Psalm 89:15-16

May 20

𝒮et today carry with it the joy of your salvation.

In moments of thought, of conversation, come back to our relationship and the price that was paid for it. Never forget that it did not come free. There is nothing more precious to Me.

Come and lay your head on My shoulder and let Me tell you stories of long ago.

Stories that will inspire you to live strong with courage and fortitude; stories found in the scriptures of David, of Moses, of Rahab, and of Mary. The Bible is full of these real-life stories of pure, raw adventure.

Your salvation is not dependent on knowing those stories. Your salvation is dependent on one thing: Jesus Christ and His death and resurrection.

But reading these stories will inspire you to walk similar lives of valor, all made possible because they had a relationship with Me. I guided and encouraged them, just as I do you, every moment of every day.

Take joy in that knowledge and join Me in the great adventure of being one with Me.

> *For everything that was written in the past was written to teach us, so that through the endurance taught in the Scriptures and the encouragement they provide we might have hope. May the God who gives endurance and encouragement give you the same attitude of mind toward each other that Christ Jesus had.*
> *Romans 15:4-5*

May 21

I will never leave you behind, My child.

I have plans for you which I am revealing slowly. If I showed you the whole picture, you would not be willing to go the difficult learning route I need to send you on to get there.

It comes back to trust.

Trust in Me as a total, fulfilling Being. Trust that I am everything and everyone you need. You may think you want something different, but I know the best way for you.

My Son is the Way, the Truth and the Life. No one comes to Me except through Him. When you know Him you know the peace that passes all understanding. You know the love that knows no bounds and you feel the trust I have asked you to live your life with.

This walk of faith is easy, beloved one. Not easy in terms of this world, but easy because you already know the outcome. The overwhelming feeling of pain and hardship you are facing is just a drop of what Jesus went through for you. It was very personal to Him. He wanted you by His side.

So never fear that I will count you as a loss, or not important enough to move a mountain for! Reach out and take My hand. I will never leave you behind.

For to this you were called, because Christ suffered for you,
leaving you an example, that you should follow His steps.
I Peter 2:21

May 22

I am here with you now. Believe Me. Trust Me.

Reach out to touch Me every moment that you think of Me. I am here with you always. You will receive all you need today and every day.

Practice My presence.

You will find so much comfort in KNOWING, not just trying to imagine or trust Me, but in KNOWING I am beside you, walking with you, helping you in the everyday decisions of life.

Please don't let go of My hand.
It is there for you always.

My love is something you will not understand until you get to Heaven.

I AM LOVE.
I don't feel love, I AM LOVE.

And My love for you is more extreme than you can even imagine.

Run in the glory of it, full speed ahead, into the vast unknown of the world, full of joy in My promises. Never fearful. My right hand will be ever before you and around you.

"Lo, I am with you always, even unto the end of the world!"
Trust in My love and My promises.

You make known to me the path of life; you will fill me
with joy in Your presence, with eternal
pleasures at Your right hand.
Psalm 16:11

May 23

I long to hold you and comfort you. Your need of Me is what I want to know and hear.

I am with you today. I am with you tomorrow. I am with you always.

But take one step at a time. You are worried about so much. Take today and deal with it today. Worry about tomorrow, tomorrow.

Be assured that I will be there to guide and comfort you every step of the way.

Trust in Me.

Lean into My arms and let go. Close your eyes and imagine yourself floating. I am holding you up. You are totally in My care.

Just let go, and I will take care of you.

Face the day with joy. The joy of My salvation. The joy of My love. The joy of communion with Me.

How beloved you are to Me!

Now, go and have joy!
The day is Mine to worry about!

But seek first His kingdom and His righteousness, and all these things will be given to you as well. Therefore, do not worry about tomorrow, for tomorrow will worry about itself. Each day has enough trouble of its own.
Matthew 6:33-34

May 24

You are scared and discouraged now. I can feel it.

Don't give up. I have an answer for you. Just wait, and trust in Me.

I long to give you the answers for your future that you so desire, but it is not in My plan to let that happen. You have to trust Me in that. Knowing would ruin everything for you. You would trust in the knowledge of the future, not in Me.

Yesterday I told you to lean back and let go, like you are floating, and I will catch you. Do it again today.

Close your eyes. Think of Me. Imagine Me next to you, holding your hand.

I will guide your every move today, if you accept it.

Are you ready? Close your eyes. Imagine it.
Reach out and touch Me. I am with My beloved child.

You will only understand this love when you get to Heaven to see Me face to face.

Until then, just float.

May the God of hope fill you with all joy and peace as you
trust in Him, so that you may overflow with hope
by the power of the Holy Spirit
Romans 15:13

May 25

These problems you have are requiring your close presence with Me. Reach out your hand and I will take it and walk with you through them.

I am a God of love.

Such love you will never understand until I hold you securely in My presence.

Every moment of the day think of Me, and I will guide you through all your decisions and problems. You have a ready helper in Me that you just need to call out for because I am

ALWAYS BY YOUR SIDE.

Face today with the challenges that it brings, with joy and love and anticipation of the future that I have planned for you. Encourage each other with words of praise. Never forget to take time to tell someone you love or care for them.

Others can feel and sense My presence in you.

What joy we will share when you stand face to face with Me! This life, with all its problems will be over, and we can rejoice in a future together.

Slip your hand into Mine now and let's walk through the day.

*Know therefore that the Lord your God is God; He is the
faithful God, keeping His covenant of love to a
thousand generations of those who love
Him and keep His commandments.*
Deuteronomy 7:9

May 26

*Y*ou are feeling My joy today. Bask in it.

It is My greatest longing to be close to you and to give you My joy and peace. Let it surround you today as you go about your daily activities. Let My presence permeate your very soul.

I AM WITH YOU.
Now, always and forever.

Today, I want you to grow more in the knowledge of Me. Study My Word. Keep your favorite verses near you and check on them often. This is how I communicate and reassure you.

Study My Word in depth to unlock the deep horizons of My love. You know I love and care for you, but go deeper.

Grow in Me. Then our relationship will go to the next level.

There is no level to My love, just a stronger sense of My presence. I am with you now and always.

Breathe a deep breath and let it out slowly knowing I will always watch over you.

Go to the next level with Me.

> *If you call out for insight and cry aloud for understanding*
> *and if you look for it as for silver and search for it as for*
> *hidden treasure, then you will understand the fear*
> *of the Lord and find the knowledge of God.*
> *Proverbs 2:3-5*

May 27

Thank you for giving up everything to Me. I am ready to catch you and help you float, trusting in Me.

Today is a new day. Face it with courage, optimism and joy, that word I always give you . . . joy. Let it permeate your soul with the knowledge of My love and care for you.

Each step you take today I will be with you, to guide you. Please take time to think about Me. I am never more than a whisper away.

Shhh. Listen to the sound of spring outside your window. Do you hear birds? They are calling out My name in praise. I love and care for them, too. I feed and clothe them, and they trust Me.

Why can't you be like them?

Just KNOW, that I will always be there to face whatever challenges this life brings. And there are many things ahead of you I wish you wouldn't have to go through. But I am there to catch you. I will never let you go alone.

Just grab My hand and walk with Me across the sand.
It can be that real . . . if you let it.

Therefore, I tell you, do not worry about your life, what you
will eat or drink; or about your body, what you will wear. Is
not life more than food, and the body more than clothes?
Look at the birds of the air; they do not sow or reap or store
away in barns, and yet your heavenly Father feeds them.
Are you not much more valuable than they?
Matthew 6:25-26

May 28

Concentrate on Me today. Try to focus on My Spirit.

Close your eyes during the day, and spend time with Me. I am in you and all around you every moment.

Never fear what is coming up. Knowing I am always with you is your best defense for whatever it is.

Together we can scale walls and climb mountains.

I need those moments with you to reinforce My presence. It is only for you that I ask this. It is not My need, but yours so that you can truly feel Me all around you.

My presence has power.
And that power will give you joy and reassurance.

Rest in it.

Have I not commanded you? Be strong and courageous. Do
not be afraid; do not be discouraged, for the Lord your
God will be with you wherever you go.
Joshua 1:9

May 29

Good morning, My child.

You are in My thoughts today.

I will surround you with My love and care.

Today will be full of surprises as you make your way through it. Surprises of love, if you look for them.

Surprises, only because I am just starting to teach you about My presence in your life.

You will start noticing little "God kisses" in things that happen, and if you are in tune with Me, you will know I sent them.

Be heartened with joy and love to share with others today.

*So then, just as you received Christ Jesus as Lord, continue
to live your lives in Him, rooted and built up in Him,
strengthened in the faith as you were taught, and
overflowing with thankfulness.
Colossians 2:6-7*

May 30

*D*ear one, you are faced with new challenges today. Listen to the still small voice inside you.

It is Me.

I am communicating with you through it. Listen carefully and follow My lead.

I will never leave you "out to dry." I will be with you in all situations, providing the answers and the way through each problem.

Later, come to Me in quiet, celebrating our time together.

Each day is precious between you and Me. Every day is numbered. Remember to walk with Me through it.

And have joy.
Inner joy.

One day we will be together and true joy and understanding will abound.

Until then, listen. Listen to My urgings.

They are My love song to you.

Teach us to number our days, that we
may gain a heart of wisdom.
Psalm 90:12

May 31

𝒟ear one, you are facing the day with warmth and love.

Know that I am with you now and always. Every moment you are awake, I am by your side, guiding you.

Take every step with the assurance of someone loved very much. This will give you the confidence you need to face every situation.

At the end of the day, think back on what happened and notice how I was with you. Remember that, and if it was special to you, write it down.

If you are discouraged another time, go back to the pages and remember how I was with you then, and know that I will be with you no matter what happens, or wherever you are.

Face the day with the courage of a much beloved child of the King!

The Spirit you received does not make you slaves, so that you live in fear again; rather, the Spirit you received brought about your adoption to sonship. And by Him we cry, "Abba, Father."
Romans 8:15

June 01

Face this day with courage and love, dear one, always looking for ways to ease the load of others. My presence in your life means that you are more aware of their needs.

You are My representative to the world.

Keep that love and assurance for you, too. If there are closed doors, do not be afraid to open them, for walking through them with Me is a new dawn, a new adventure.

You never know where I am going to lead you, but the new path will lead you closer to Me.

Let Me hold you in My arms this morning.
Close your eyes and feel My love surround you.

Remember this moment through the day and draw strength from it.

I pray that the eyes of your heart may be enlightened in order
that you may know the hope to which He has called you, the
riches of His glorious inheritance in His holy people, and
His incomparably great power for us who believe.
Ephesians 1:18-19

June 02

The end or beginning of a week, the beginning or the end of a month. These things represent time.

I look at time much differently than you. I look at time as a bridge between you and Me.

Cross over the bridge this morning, My love.

Take My hand and step into My world. Together we will be free of the problems and pain you are going through. No more loneliness.

Come with Me.
Breathe My love in deeply.

Hold My hand as we smile and laugh and run through grassy pastures together.

When time necessitates you to let go of My hand and return to your world, use this experience to trust Me and remember that I am ever with you and around you with a passionate love for you, My precious child.

This is My gift to you this morning.

The Lord is my strength and my shield; my heart trusts in
Him, and He helps me. My heart leaps for joy,
and with my song I praise Him.
Psalm 28:7

June 03

*Y*ou are here with Me this morning.

Take My hand and let's wander through time again. Let's see where we can go if you remain connected to Me.

All the things in your past are behind you now.

What remains is only a memory, whether happy or sad. I have given you peace over them, even the most painful ones.

Look ahead to the future now, for your connection with Me is of utmost importance. Together we will fly through time, ending up at the Father's seat of Mercy.

Take one step at a time, knowing I am beside you. Face today's challenges with total and utter confidence, for you are an heir of My love.

Hold your head high, breathe deep and
face today with courage!

You will keep in perfect peace those whose minds
are steadfast, because they trust in You.
Isaiah 26:3

June 04

Good morning, precious child. You are here with Me now.

How many times I have longed to hold you in My arms but you keep stepping away!

Come and let Me enfold you into My arms so that you can feel the warmth of My love.

This sacred connection between us is My gift for you, never farther away than your thoughts. Use it to climb to the highest possibilities of your goals.

I have given you a vision of what I want you to accomplish here on earth.

With the strength and power of the love connection between us, you can do anything.

Go forward today with that knowledge.

When you were dead in your sins and in the uncircumcision of your flesh, God made you alive with Christ. He forgave us all our sins, having canceled the charge of our legal indebtedness, which stood against us and condemned us; He has taken it away, nailing it to the cross.
Colossians 2:13-14

June 05

The morning is singing My praises again through the birds. The whole of creation is calling forth My Name.

Let your lips and your heart honor Me in this way.

Forever I have called you by name. You were always going to be. I have loved you with an everlasting love. Take this love with you throughout the day and share it with others.

Only through that love can they find the hope they all seek in their deepest souls. My Holy Spirit will enable you to touch their souls with that love.

It's a joyous day to be alive here. Many horrible things are happening all around you, but today, between you and I, there is peace and joy.

Rejoice in it.

Draw strength from it.

*But from everlasting to everlasting the Lord's love is with
those who fear Him, and His righteousness with their
children's children-with those who keep His
covenant and remember to obey His precepts.
Psalms 103:17-18*

June 06

I am here with you now, My beloved child. Rest in that assurance.

Today will have many issues to be dealt with. Don't get so bogged down with them that you forget to seek Me, for I am always right there beside you.

My love for you cannot be measured in words but in the day-to-day direction I give you.

I love you so much that I sent My Son to die for you. Could you do that if you didn't know someone?

That is the proof that I know you, and that I love you more than you can even begin to understand.

I know every hair on your head, and I love every one of them! I know every problem you are going through. They are not easy, but they are ways to draw you closer to Me. Walk through them with Me.

Think of Jesus' death on the cross as My personal gift to only you. Yes, I would have done that if you were the only person in the entire world.

I will always love and take care of you.
Let's walk through these issues together.

You see, at just the right time, when we were still powerless, Christ died for the ungodly. Very rarely will anyone die for a righteous person, though for a good person someone might possibly dare to die. But God demonstrates His own love for us in this: While we were still sinners, Christ died for us.
Romans 5:6-8

June 07

Open your heart to Me, dear one.

I can take you where you have never been before. Together we can soar through the clouds of your highest dreams.

I have given you those dreams, those visions, of the person I want you to be . . .

the person I know you can be.

Whatever limitations you think this earth puts on you are gone when you hold My hand.

I have no limitations. My world is endless.

Fly with Me today, over the hills, the cities, over your problems and limitations. Together we will reach your highest dreams.

Just don't let go of My hand. It is your lifeline.

Close your eyes. Take My hand

Here we go . . .

See what great love the Father has lavished on us, that we
should be called children of God! And that is what we
are! The reason the world does not know us
is that it did not know Him.
I John 3:1

June 08

Dear one, don't fret over the small things in your life.

Today is a day of new possibilities with Me. What seems huge to you is only small in My world.

Take on My world and let Me handle it.

I want you to focus on Me, on My presence in your life, every moment.

Rise with Me above the clouds, above your problems. I will give you that strength.

In Me alone you will have that courage.

Your courage will be a silent testimony of our relationship. Silent in your heart but screaming towards the devil.

You have obtained victory, dear one.

You are Mine and all heaven rejoices!

Jesus looked at them and said, "With man this is impossible,
but not with God; all things are possible with God."
Mark 10:27

June 09

*C*ome to Me in the stillness of your mind.

Reach for Me from the depths of your soul. Stand ready to march ahead with Me to the battle I have prepared for you.

Together we can do it!

Have you ever wondered why I put you where you are? I put you there at this time and in this place because I have called you as My own. I have chosen you to carry out My work exactly where you are among the people you work with, your friends and your family.

They need to see Me in you, the Me that only you and your personality bring.

I have filled you with an everlasting love. Share it with others. Bring them home to Me.

You are My beloved child of whom I am so proud.

Have joy in that, in the very depths of your soul.

As for God, His way is perfect: the Lord's word is flawless;
He shields all who take refuge in Him. For who is God
besides the Lord? And who is the Rock except our God? It is
God who arms me with strength and keeps my way secure.
2 Samuel 22:31-33

June 10

So many times in this life My people lose sight of the vision I have given them. Whether from fear or problems, they give up too easily. Keep striving towards the goal I have given you.

You know what that goal is, from the bottom of your heart.
Don't give it up.

Let Me hold your hand, keeping you focused and balanced as we accomplish the mission. Look neither to the right or to the left.

Look only to Me, the source of your strength and your salvation.

Today is a new day with new opportunities I will place in front of you. Don't be weak, for I have armed you with strong armor, if you would just put it on!

How we will rejoice over this time when we see each other face to face!

Keep going, dear one.
Your Beloved is close beside you now.

I WILL NOT LET YOU FALL.

Therefore, put on the full armor of God, so that when the day
of evil comes, you may be able to stand your ground, and
after you have done everything, to stand.
Ephesians 6:13

June 11

$\mathscr{I}$ am the God of miracles in your life.

Miracles that will be used to bless others, to touch their lives so that they will know of My great love for them. And miracles for you, dear one.

Expect them today, knowing that I will be there to provide and care for you.

Just letting go and trusting Me is a gift from Me to you. It may seem hard at first, but the more you do it, the easier it becomes.

Believe, dear one, that I am with you, for I am.

I am beside you, waiting for you to reach out your hand to Me. Take it now, for you will never feel such love.

Close your eyes and reach out and touch Me. I am with you now. Your fears will fade when you realize and envision My presence with you.

Let's start the day together now.

Expect a miracle!

Your ways, God, are holy. What god is as great as our God?
You are the God who performs miracles; You display
Your power among the peoples. With Your mighty
arm You redeemed Your people, the
descendants of Jacob and Joseph.
Psalms 77:13-15

June 12

Sometimes things in your daily life seem very difficult. But if you realize that I am ALWAYS beside you, it will be much easier to go through.

Walk with Me through the sands of time. Travel back through history to stories of how I conquered giants and parted waters and rose people from the dead.

The Friend Who walks with you today is that same God.

I am all-powerful and I am all-love.

When you take My hand, an electric current passes through from Me to you, connecting us.

You have this power, beloved. Let me clothe you early in the day with My protective armor of love and righteousness. I am smiling at My child now because you are allowing Me to care for you.

Even though I am your "Abba," I am still the God of the universe.

You are blessed. Walk with Me today.

Then I thought, "To this I will appeal: the years when the Most High stretched out His right hand. I will remember the deeds of the Lord; yes, I will remember Your miracles of long ago. I will consider all Your works and meditate on all Your mighty deeds."
Psalm 77:10-12

June 13

Dear child, I feel your tension now.

Rest in the knowledge of My extreme love for you. It is more, so much more, than you can even begin to understand.

If you fall, I am here beside you, ready to catch you at a moment's notice. Close your eyes and rest in Me a moment. You will draw peace from it.

Breathe in My love and My presence deeply into your soul.

Armed with Me, you can face anything. I have great plans for you if you will let Me lead you to them.

Come with Me now into the day. Don't let go of My hand. When you don't sense Me, close your eyes and breathe deeply.

I am here.

In You, Lord, I have taken refuge; let me never be put to shame; deliver me in Your righteousness. Turn Your ear to me, come quickly to my rescue; be my Rock of refuge, a strong fortress to save me.
Psalm 31:1-2

June 14

You feel like you have strayed away from Me because you have not been spending deep time with Me. You have been praying, but not taking the time to really come apart and "listen" to My still small voice in your soul.

It is not "straying", because you are My child, but our relationship suffers when you talk to Me but don't take the time to listen.

Listen to Me, beloved one.

I have My arms around you, and I am whispering in your ear. You are missing so much! What I want to share with you is the joy I feel at having you as My child.

Let Me infuse your soul with laughter!

Make the decision every morning, and during the worst of times to say, "I choose You!", then carve out some time to come apart with Me to listen and learn.

The peace inside your soul will be your sign that My presence is strongly with you.

Don't let the world and its busyness cause you to stray. You are Mine and I am yours.

Come see what that means!

Since You are my Rock and my fortress, for the sake of Your name lead and guide me. Keep me free from the trap that is set for me, for You are my refuge. Into Your hands I commit my spirit; deliver me, Lord, my faithful God.
Psalm 31:3-5

June 15

Oh, what a glorious morning on the earth!

Amidst all the pain, a new dawn is always new hope. Hope for those who truly love and serve Me.

Today is filled with a pocketful of surprises that I have in store for you, ones that will give you joy. Smile and know that I am with you when they happen.

Take My hand and walk with Me through the day, stopping to praise Me often. A peace will come over you when you do. Smile, for you and I will be sharing the deepest moment of togetherness.

You are My beloved child and I long for such communion with you.

The world ahead is full of unrest. The future will not be easy for My children. That is why spending more time in deeper communion with Me is your strength.

Never let go of My hand, for I AM ALWAYS WITH YOU.

My heart, O God, is steadfast, my heart is steadfast; I will sing and make music. Awake, my soul! Awake, harp and lyre! I will awaken the dawn. I will praise You, Lord, among the nations; I will sing of You among the peoples.
Psalm 57:7-9

June 16

Oh, child, you are in My embrace this morning. Never doubt and never fear. I am close beside you now and always.

If you do not always feel My presence, it is because you have allowed the world to push Me away. Television, the internet, loud music: these are just a few of the things that make deeper communion with Me challenging.

Take time to put Me on in the morning.

Allow Me to don the full armor of righteousness, love and joy on you. Wear it with pride. Hold your head up like the child of the King that you are. Together we can face whatever challenges are ahead. I hunger for these quiet moments between us where I can infuse you with My love.

Imagine you are hooked up to an IV, with healthy blood filling every part of your body. Come and connect with Me and let Me send through you the infusion of My love to every part of your being.

Imagine how you will feel when My love is coursing through your veins!! Oh, dear one, so much is available to you if you will but allow it!

Come to Me now.

Stand firm then, with the belt of truth buckled around your waist, with the breastplate of righteousness in place, and with your feet fitted with the readiness that comes from the gospel of peace. In addition to this, take up the shield of faith, with which you can extinguish all the flaming arrows of the evil one. Take the helmet of salvation and the sword of the Spirit, which is the Word of God.
Ephesians 6:14-17

June 17

ll the earth is filled with My glory.

From the rising of the sun until its setting, My glory shines over all.
You have but to open your eyes to see it and to think of Me.

But you go through life without stopping to praise Me, without
stopping to call out My name for your deepest wounds. You go
through life as if it were all about you and making the "mighty" dollar.

Don't you know I have the whole world in My hand? And that you are
My child?

You are My heir.

Free yourself of the world and come live in My world where you are
aware of My love and presence, where you stop to wonder at the
beauty of the majestic rose, gaze upon the magnificent mountain, the
beautiful stream, and the tiny bird.

Sense Me. Be aware.
I am here, there and everywhere.

Wherever you are, I AM.

This is the real world. Come and walk with Me in it.

*Praise be to the Lord God, the God of Israel, who alone does
marvelous deeds. Praise be to His glorious name forever;
may the whole earth be filled with His glory.*
Psalm 72:18-19

June 18

Are you scared this morning? Don't you know I am with you?

Close your eyes and sense My presence. Feel My peace drop over you like a blanket.

Today is a sacred day between you and Me. It will be the day you remember that I walked with you. You can make it happen. We can be that close. Others crowd around but it is My relationship with you that keeps you focused.

I am the Master of the universe, Maker of Heaven and Earth. Where would you be but for Me? Yet I have chosen you, just you, to be with Me.

I long for intimate time with you. Please spend it with Me now. Read My word. Let Me speak to you of past glories and past stories, and over all, My love for you through all existence. It is the written story through all generations, ending with the story of your salvation through My Son, Jesus Christ.

Let's make our own story.
The story of how I walked with you . . . just you.

I am here, dear one. I am here.

> *The Spirit of the Sovereign Lord is on Me, because the Lord*
> *has anointed Me to proclaim good news to the poor, and*
> *provide for those who grieve in Zion to bestow on them*
> *a crown of beauty instead of ashes, the oil of joy*
> *instead of mourning, and a garment of praise*
> *instead of a spirit of despair.*
> *Isaiah 61:1, 3*

June 19

How do you face the profound sadness of some days? By keeping your mind focused on Me.

I am, oh, so aware of the pain and confusion that you feel, the not understanding of why some things happen. It is hard to make you understand while you are in this world. Just know that someday you will know and see things the way I do.

Use this time to let Me fold you into My arms and hold you closely. Close your eyes and put your head against My chest. I long to hold you like this until your pain subsides.

When the pain comes back, return to My embrace, drawing strength from My nearness and absolute love for you.

I understand the suffering you are going through, more than you will ever know. When I walked the earth, I loved those around Me, yet My love was rejected. My words and actions were criticized, and I was abandoned and horribly murdered. Yet, when I rose again, I was able to show love in the face of it all.

The One that has been through it all is here with you now, wanting to love you with an everlasting love. Let Me draw you into My arms so you may feel the strength of it and be able to face another day here.

Take heart. I am here, and I will come again.
Just for now, rest in My embrace.

So do not fear, for I am with you; do not be dismayed, for I am your God. I will strengthen you and help you; I will uphold you with My righteous right hand.
Isaiah 41:10

June 20

Child, I am here with you now. Close your eyes and feel My presence. Draw My closeness in with every breath.

During the day, find a quiet room and do this. These moments with Me will give you the strength you need to carry through.

When you feel tempted to draw away from Me by the busyness of life, come back to your quiet place, and close your eyes and draw Me in with every breath.

Today will be a wonderful day for us. Face it with courage and joy. The little things in your life need to be done with as much fervor as the big things, as I have appointed them all to you.

Keep your eyes focused on the dream I have given you. With Me beside you, we can accomplish it, even when others say we can't. There are no "no's" in My world.

The vision I gave you is the vision I will give you the strength and knowledge to fulfill. Seek only to do My will and we will accomplish it.

And when you feel like you've reached your limit and can't go further? Find that quiet place again, close your eyes, and breathe Me in.

I will surround you with My love and strength.

To humans belong the plans of the heart, but from the Lord comes the proper answer of the tongue. Commit to the Lord whatever you do, and He will establish your plans. The Lord works everything out to its proper end.
Proverbs 16:1, 3-4

June 21

I am really here with you now.

You are learning to sense My presence. The world seems far away as you read this. I am surrounding you with My armor, protecting you and our time together.

You and Me. Me and You.

Together we can do this.

Since before the foundation of the earth, I knew about you, and planned for you: when you would come, and where you and your family and friends would live.

I love you with an everlasting love.

There is no one more special to Me than you. Let My love and comfort and surround you today.

We are together.

You and Me, Me and you.

I will praise the Lord, who counsels me; even at night my
heart instructs me. I keep my eyes always on the Lord.
With Him at my right hand, I will not be shaken.
Psalm 16:7-8

June 22

*D*o you ever wonder why there is so much pain and suffering in the world? Do you think about how a God who loves so much allows it? Oh, child, the pain to Me is worse than the pain you see and feel.

Only through pain will people come to realize that this earth is not their home. This earth and the life on it that they think they like so much is but a drop in the hat of what I have in store for them if they would just look to Me. In their pain, I long for them to reach out to Me, to see life as deeper than their day-to-day trials.

One day it will be different. The pain and suffering will be wiped away. Pain and evil will be gone, and we will live forever in peace and joy.

Choose righteousness, child. Amid everything, choose righteousness and peace. I am at the heart of it all.

"Joy cometh in the morning."
You will see. I will lead you through it.

No matter how much pain you are going through, don't let go of My hand. I will lead you like a shepherd through the dark valleys and high mountains. Don't look down or let go. Joy is ahead.

You see just a glimmer now, but soon it will surround you with bursts of light. Oh, how I look forward to that moment!

Don't ever let go.

For His anger lasts only a moment, but His favor lasts
a lifetime; weeping may stay for the night, but
rejoicing comes in the morning.
Psalm 30:5

June 23

Good morning, dear child. Today is a day of new possibilities.

Close your eyes and be filled with My joy, for I am right here beside you.

Oh, the love I have for you, the joy I long to share with you! Fill yourself up with My presence and we will face the world together.

This world is in such turmoil, but you needn't be. I have given you the promise of My abiding care and guidance. This should allow you to face even the grimmest predictions and problems with peace.

The "peace that passes all understanding."

Let others be amazed at the peacefulness of your countenance during such times. You have the Holy One on your side. What possibly can you fear?

So, gather yourself together this morning, wrapped up in the knowledge of My love, and face today with your head held high.

I will be beside you all the way!

Do not be anxious about anything, but in every situation, by prayer and petition, with thanksgiving, present your requests to God. And the peace of God, which transcends all understanding, will guard your hearts and your minds in Christ Jesus.
Philippians 4:6-7

June 24

I long to speak to you in the quiet moments.

Did you leave the busyness of your life yesterday to come apart and commune with Me? You would have drawn so much strength from it if you did.

Today, put one foot in front of the other and just plow ahead. I have a special task for you that only you will know of. If you allow Me to guide you, I can fulfill a ministry in you just by your daily walk. Others will be blessed.

So much I want to tell you is in My written Word. The Bible is your guide to live a complete life with Me. Stories of how I led the Israelites, of how I led Paul, and personal promises to you of how I will lead you.

These are hints of the closeness I long to have with you.

Carry it with you when possible to read words directly from Me to you. Let it warm your very being. Then close your eyes, and think of Me, for the very same God of the Bible is right beside you, longing to love you.

Just put one foot in front of the other. This will be a great day!!

Now may the God of peace, who through the blood of the
eternal covenant brought back from the dead our Lord Jesus,
that great Shepherd of the sheep, equip you with everything
good for doing His will, and may He work in us what is
pleasing to Him, through Jesus Christ, to Whom
be glory for ever and ever. Amen.
Hebrews 13:20-21

June 25

You are here with Me now, dear one, and nothing is more precious to Me.

Reach out and touch My hand. I am that close.

Today will be a day of victories for you. Victories you may not see yet, but in your walk with Me, they happen.

Behind the scenes the real battles are going on as evil pulls and pushes at you. But if you put on My breastplate of righteousness in the morning, I arm you with the protection against it.

Someday you will know. I will tell you of the fascinating things that you could not see through your earthly eyes. The battles are real, dear one, and I long to protect you with My armor. The evil everywhere cannot touch you when you wear it.

When you first arise, come to Me and but ask for it. I will surround you with the protection.

Let Me take care of you, for you are so precious to Me.

"Today you are going into battle against your enemies. Do not be fainthearted or afraid; do not panic or be terrified by them. For the Lord your God is the one who goes with you to fight for you against your enemies to give you victory."
Deuteronomy 20:3-4

June 26

In the stillness of the morning, you sense My presence more.

Some people stay up very late and don't take the time in the morning to commune with Me. They are missing so much!

Starting the day with Me is allowing Me to protect you when I cover you with My armor of righteousness. Wear it proudly. Feel its weight. Know it is My love that has "cocooned" you.

I am smiling because there is joy in our communion. Such joy when you come to Me fresh out of bed!

Fall on your knees and wait until My presence settles over you. There you are at the threshold of the kingdom of God, kneeling at My throne.

I hear your prayers, dear one, for I am right beside you. Such reverence is precious to Me.

Pour out your heart and your soul, for the King of the universe hears and will answer your prayers.

Then rise up and get ready for the day.

Because you have given Me permission to cover you with the protection of My love, all things are possible, if you will but believe.

> *He will stand and shepherd his flock in the strength of the*
> *Lord, in the majesty of the name of the Lord his God.*
> *And they will live securely, for then his greatness*
> *will reach to the ends of the earth.*
> *Micah 5:4*

June 27

Do you ever wonder where I really am? Being omnipresent, I am everywhere. The only thing I want you to understand about that is that I am always with you, My chosen child.

Does it bother you when I say you are chosen? Since before the creation of the world, I knew of you and chose you to be My own.

No matter your background, or even if your mother or father made you feel unloved or unwanted, I planned you. I made you. I CHOSE YOU to be Mine, to walk with Me, to be My beloved child.

Yes, you will fall. And no, you will never, ever be deserving. But it doesn't matter because Christ paid the cost for our relationship. Oh, the pain of those days! The pain of seeing Him who rules with Me going through such agony and pain at the hands of those We loved.

Days pass much faster for Me than for you, but those days passed SO slowly . . . But such joy when it was over! Now the world can know of the victory We have over the devil!

I could not have paid for you with anything more precious to Me than My dear Son, Jesus Christ.

Come near. You are deeply loved.

And I pray that you, being rooted and established in love,
may have power, together with all the Lord's holy people, to
grasp how wide and long and high and deep is the love of
Christ, and to know this love that surpasses knowledge that
you may be filled to the measure of all the fullness of God.
Ephesians 3:17-19

June 28

*G*ood morning, child of Mine.

How the earth sings My glory if you could but understand its language!

It involves trust on your part to acknowledge it.

The birds do it constantly. They live such simple lives, yet it is in simplicity that they learn to glorify Me. I provide food and shelter for them, and they are grateful.

Do you know I provide food and shelter for you? I have opened doors for jobs, for opportunities, for education. I have guided your life much more than you could ever realize here on this earth.

Because of Me, I have allowed you to "own" the land your house is on, or the furniture in your apartment.

It is all Mine. You are but a sojourner here.

"In My Father's house are many mansions," Jesus said. Soon you will share in the riches of Heaven with Us. But while you are here on earth, take time to be like a bird, trusting Me to take care of you, and stopping to give Me praise often!

"Do not let your hearts be troubled. You believe in God, believe also in Me. My Father's house has many rooms; if that were not so, would I have told you that I am going there to prepare a place for you? And if I go and prepare a place for you, I will come back and take you to be with Me that you also may be where I am."
John 14:1-3

June 29

*O*h, how the morning sings of My glory! I have set you in it to observe and to learn how to praise Me in all situations, for I am the Lord your God.

My love for you needs to be returned in following My commands and obeying Me. When we see each other face to face, you will understand all I went through to make you Mine.

Return My love, dear one.

Come to Me and imagine My presence. Let Me fill you with an everlasting love. Serve Me and praise Me. You will find much joy.

Ever since the creation of the world I have planned this day. It is a day in which you will shine.

Rise up with Me and reach to the sky! Jump for joy, for you and I together will conquer all the unseen evil around you!

Every day is a new battle which you don't see. I see, and I know. I need you to stay close to My presence to overcome.

I have shielded you from so much. One day you will look back at all this and truly understand.

Until then, take My hand and walk with Me.

Sing to Him, sing praise to Him; tell of all His wonderful acts. Glory in His holy name; let the hearts of those who seek the Lord rejoice. Look to the Lord and His strength; seek His face always.
I Chronicles 16:9-11

June 30

When the turbulence is great, when your troubles seem so heavy, call out My Name. A shaft of light will pierce your being and I will dwell in you.

Surround yourself with thoughts of Me, of peace and joy. Where there is peace, I AM. Where there is pain, I AM. Through your darkest moments and through times of happy surprises, I AM there.

Dear one, My desire is to have you be conscious of Me wherever you are. I am always conscious of you. I will not let one moment of your life go by without My knowing.

I am truly the Good Shepherd in that I am always guiding you. Only when you turn your back on Me do I allow you to walk alone. When you do, I watch you with great sadness as you leave Me to go out and live a life of worldly pleasures. How I long for you to return!

When even the smallest thought of Me is expressed, I fold you into My loving arms again. All of the mistakes you made on your own, I work with to help you, and to help others. This is just a small sample of My love for you.

Do not turn away, dear one. For we can accomplish so much more if you will let Me guide you always.

I have so many wonders in store for you!!

And He who searches our hearts knows the mind of the Spirit, because the Spirit intercedes for God's people in accordance with the will of God. And we know that in all things God works for the good of those who love Him, who have been called according to His purpose.
Romans 8:27-28

July 01

My lightness waits for you this morning. Don My presence and let it shine for others to see.

Throughout the day, seek out time with Me. You will never regret these moments.

I am so glad you are here with Me now. Close your eyes and envision Me beside you.

"Taste and see that the Lord is good", David said. He walked with Me in a very real way. He was able to sense My presence and knew wherever He was, he was near to Me, and I to him.

David did not live a perfect life. Many times, he turned his back on Me, hurting Me and others, but he always came back, and we walked together. He is with Me now.

Beloved, be like David.
In the morning, seek My face, and sing My praise.

I will be your stronghold. I always have been. I want you to be more aware of it and of Me.

Let Me be your strength and focus today, My beloved one.

Taste and see that the Lord is good; Blessed is the one who takes refuge in Him.
Psalm 34:8

July 02

Child of Mine, you are here with Me now. You have stopped the clock in your busy schedule to spend some time with Me.

I will draw close to you, as close as you allow Me to. Together we can do great things for My Kingdom. You may think them small things, but seeds have been planted that I will continue watering over the years.

In Heaven you will see the whole story.

What a day of rejoicing that will be! You will sit at My feet and visualize the stories of what was really happening in this world.

If only you could see now! The evil is real, dear one, but you have overcome it. Every time you call out My Name, we have the victory. Always.

I reign supreme and nothing can ever stand up to Me.

So, come to Me in the morning and spend these precious moments with Me. Do not lose your focus. There is a battle to be won, but you have just overcome!

Smile with Me, My child, for you are loved.

Now this I know: The Lord gives victory to His anointed. He answers him from His heavenly sanctuary with the victorious power of His right hand.
Psalm 20:6

July 03

Dear child of Mine, take My hand and let Me walk with you through time, a walk with Me into the past where the Bible comes alive again.

There is no greater history than that which I commanded into being. Every flower, every tree, every animal, I put into being. Each was designed not only for need, but for beauty.

Those who do not know Me can look at My creations and know of My existence. There is no possibility that even one of those marvelous creatures or creations could have just "happened".

When you get discouraged by things in your life, take time to walk with Me and study nature around you.

I had a plan. I made it, and you are a very important part of that plan.

Take each day one step at a time, putting one foot in front of the other. I will never leave you.

The proof is all around you.

The heavens declare the glory of God; the
skies proclaim the work of His hands.
Psalm 19:1

July 04

By faith your forefathers walked with Me. By faith, you are walking with Me now.

Enoch sought Me every morning when he woke up. His hearing was so fine-tuned that he could listen to My urgings and I took him up to Heaven to be with Me.

I long for us to have that closeness, for you to desire to walk with Me as fervently as Enoch did. The joy you would experience is beyond that which you could ever envision.

This world is not a real place. It is a testing ground between evil and good.

The real life is the one we will share after you have left this place and I have come to bring you to Me. Only then will you experience My true love, joy, peace and praise, things which now you can only take by faith.

But it is real, and it awaits you.

Come and sense a portion of it now. Walk with Me like Enoch did.

Take My hand and but ask, for I am there.

By faith Enoch was taken from this life, so that he did not experience death: "He could not be found, because God had taken him away." For before he was taken, he was commended as one who pleased God.
Hebrews 11:5

July 05

I am near you, dear child. I will rain the Holy Spirit upon you so that your heart and mind will be opened to receive Me.

It is My desire that you have asked for this closeness. Just rest in the knowledge that I am here.

You may sing praises to Me and learn of Me, and I will bless you, dear one.

How I long for our hearts to be intertwined in each other's!

Soon, My dear one, soon.
Until that time, I will be ever near you and I will take care of you.

You never need to fear.

Let My Spirit come upon you now. Close your eyes and imagine My presence, for I am there with you now no matter what.

It is My joy to have you seek Me.

But I am like an olive tree flourishing in the house of God; I trust in God's unfailing love for ever and ever. For what You have done I will always praise You in the presence of Your faithful people. And I will hope in Your name, for Your name is good.
Psalm 52:8-9

July 06

In the stillness of the morning, I will come to you. You never need to be afraid if you believe in Me.

I know you believe, but you still have fears inside of you.

Practice My presence. You have felt it before. Remember. Write out our times of closeness and miracles so that you will call it to mind when you don't understand a situation and your faith is weak. The memory will encourage you.

I only ask you to go by faith a little longer. Soon you will understand everything important. Until then, I want you to know that I am truly with you.

When Jesus returned to Heaven to be with Me, He promised that He would come back again. And until that time, We sent the Holy Spirit to guide you. We work together as One because of Our love for you.

Some might call us the "Dream Team."

But We are not a dream, dear one. We are the Lovers of your soul, and our greatest desire is to have you dwell in Heaven with us, a victor from this current life.

Have faith. We have already overcome the world. There is nothing to fear. Ease your soul with what you know and have experienced.

> *"I have told you these things, so that in Me you may have*
> *peace. In this world you will have trouble. But take*
> *heart! I have overcome the world!*
> *John 16:33*

July 07

Entwine your soul with Mine. Come and let Me take you places you have never dared to go before.

Rise up and take My hand, and together we will fly through space and time. I want you to truly see where Jesus walked, where He lived and died for you.

Envision His life and His death. Come to accept the love We have for you. It should permeate your everyday life, helping you to face your earthly challenges head on knowing you are the beloved child for whom so much was sacrificed.

Close your eyes and imagine His anguished eyes looking at you with love and determination as the nails were driven into His feet and hands. This should let you know how much you are loved.

Live your life today as if every moment were the last.

Stay connected to Me as your lifeline. We have already overcome the world.

You have nothing to fear, and only joy to look forward to.

I have been crucified with Christ and I no longer live, but
Christ lives in me. The life I now live in the body, I
live by faith in the Son of God, who loved
me and gave Himself for me.
Galatians 2:20

July 08

Come to Me, My child, and let Me ease your fears.

No matter how many times I have reassured you and shown you miracles of My love and care for you, you are still afraid to really let go, to really believe.

Fall back into My arms and let Me guide you as you float through time and space.

I will never let go, dear one.
I will always be there to guide and hold you.

Your troubles that seem so huge, are just momentary things. Keep your eyes on Me, the Author of your salvation, the one true Love of your very being.

I will never ever let you go.
I love you too much.

Let us draw near to God with a sincere heart and with the full assurance that faith brings, having our hearts sprinkled to cleanse us from a guilty conscience and having our bodies washed with pure water. Let us hold unswervingly to the hope we profess, for He who promised is faithful.
Hebrews 10:22-23

July 09

I am here, dear one, and I know your needs so well. I have been hurting along with you.

This is all so hard for you to understand, but it is all in My plan which will unfold soon. Every step you have taken has been very important in your growth. It is carefully mapped out by Me.

Just trust Me.

I know you don't like it, but I am molding your character. You are growing in Me and we are growing so much closer than if you were happily going through life with no problems.

Yes, I have a plan, and it is for us. I will take care of you. You will see.

Just trust Me.

What is in your future? It is better that I not tell you that, but what is important for you to know is that you and I will be growing closer together. Your life will be changed, and others will be affected by our teaming together.

Don't be depressed, dear one.
There is joy ahead in Me.

> *In all this you greatly rejoice, though now for a little while*
> *you may have had to suffer grief in all kinds of trials. These*
> *have come so that the proven genuineness of your faith - of*
> *greater worth than gold, which perishes even though*
> *refined by fire - may result in praise, glory and*
> *honor when Jesus Christ is revealed.*
> *I Peter 1:6-7*

July 10

$\mathcal{D}$o not be afraid of the future.

Do not be afraid of today, or tomorrow. For I am with you, waiting for you to take My hand, giving Me free rein to guide you through your problems.

Remember yesterday. If you stayed close to Me, we had a victorious day. If you chose to go through the day alone, you experienced loneliness and fear.

No matter what happened yesterday, if you choose to walk with Me today, I will turn disasters into benefits, mistakes into second chances.

You can't lose, dear one, if you choose Me.

The world may live to its own dying heartbeat, but where you and I dwell is love and light and joy and hope, all made possible by the death and resurrection of Jesus.

It's not much of a choice, is it? But I have to let you make it.

I am here.

And He who searches our hearts knows the mind of the
Spirit, because the Spirit intercedes for God's people in
accordance with the will of God. And we know that in all
things God works for the good of those who love Him,
who have been called according to His purpose.
Romans 8:27-28

July 11

Oh, child of Mine, child of the King, you are blessed this morning! I love you with an everlasting love.

Come and let Me fold you into My arms until you feel secure again.

Walk through the day with your head held high. Though problems teem around you, you have a link to Me that enables you to tackle each one with assurance.

No matter what happens, I am never far from you.

Remember that often through the day. Strengthen our link by closing your eyes and calling My name.

Imagine Me right beside you, for I am, now and always.

I will be with you to walk through troubles, through pain, through fear and through joy. You are My creation, My created being, one who I made just for Me.

Together we can do anything!

The Lord is my light and my salvation - whom shall I fear?
The Lord is the stronghold of my life - of whom shall I
be afraid? For in the day of trouble He will keep me safe
in His dwelling; He will hide me in the shelter of His
sacred tent and set me high upon a rock.
Psalm 27:1, 5

July 12

Where are your thoughts this morning? Are they focused on Me? You will draw so much strength from Me if they are.

I will take you to fly over the mountains and valleys of life. Your connection with Me allows that. Like Peter, only when you fear and look down will you lose your way.

Keep focused on Me and trust Me. I will never let you down.

I know you are scared inside. Please don't be, My child. I express over and over to you every moment of the day how I will always take care of you.

Can you think of something that happened yesterday that made you smile? Something that you felt was a miracle, large or small?

It was Me.

As you grow deeper in our relationship, you will become more and more aware of how I bless and guide you constantly.

I look forward to your growth towards Me! What joy you will experience!

Hang on, dear one. We're going up!

> *"Come," He said. Then Peter got down out of the boat, walked on the water and came toward Jesus. But when he saw the wind, he was afraid and, beginning to sink, cried out, "Lord, save me!" Immediately Jesus reached out His hand and caught him. "You of little faith," He said, "why did you doubt?"*
> *Matthew 14:29-31*

July 13

*I*n the darkest moments of your life, I am beside you.

When your soul cries out in pain, I am there, longing for you to call out to Me so I can come and fold you into My arms.

This connection we have is so precious to Me. It is the reason I made you.

My joy is made complete when you reach out for Me.

The world is teeming with evil, beloved, and I long to shield you from it. But I have chosen not to take you out of it yet. There is so much to learn.

You may think you cannot go even one step further. It is too much.

It is not, dear one. With Me you can face anything. If you have total trust in Me for the abiding knowledge of My love, you will know, really know, that whatever happens will be okay if you stay close to Me.

Reach up now and take My hand. Together we can scale this mountain, walk through this valley.

You are with the God of the universe.
Look up, dear one. Look up.

As the deer pants for streams of water, so my soul pants for
You, my God. My soul thirsts for God, for the living God.
When can I go and meet with God? Put your hope in God,
for I will yet praise Him, my Savior and my God.
Psalm 42:1-2, 5

July 14

Like a mother hen, I long to gather My little ones under My wings, but you were not interested.

You are now, and I am so thankful.

I love to spend time with you. As you go about your busy day, think of these moments with Me because I am there with you always, longing to be closer. Just like you want to be close to Me sometimes, I ALWAYS want to be close to you.

Face the day with strength, and when you have fears or worries, lean on Me.

I AM HERE WITH YOU ALWAYS.

I do not want to tell you the future, which you think you want to know. It is far better for you not to. I need you to gently trust in Me. I will guide you. There would be no lessons learned, no utter dependence on Me, if I let you know the future. Just make sure to ask for My direction. Then I can lead you.

The future is bright for you. I have something very special planned. Just don't let go. When you doubt, go into that quiet place you have discovered and call My name.

I will surround you in My peace, joy and love.

But You, Lord, are a shield around me, my Glory, the One
who lifts my head high. I call out to the Lord, and He
answers me from His holy mountain.
Psalm 3:3-4

July 15

I know you are discouraged because I am leading you on a different path than you thought.

Where are you in your trust in Me? I will comfort you each step of the way. I have a plan for you. Just put your faith in Me and we will walk a glorious path here together.

Each step you take I have planned for you. You don't know what it is, but I do. And I have promised over and over to take care of you.

Just don't let go.

I AM WITH YOU.

You see things very differently than Me. I am asking you for growth in our relationship. Real growth.

I am pleased with you in what you have given up for Me when I asked you to. I will not forget.

You are truly My child. I will help you.

Just call out My name.

There is much power in that.

For in Christ all the fullness of the Deity lives in bodily form,
and in Christ you have been brought to fullness. He is the
Head over every power and authority.
Colossians 2:9-10

July 16

$\mathcal{I}$ want you to trust in Me. To know I am with you when you wake up and when you sleep.

I know you have many problems in life. Cast them upon Me and I will help you through them.

Have joy, unbridled joy in My presence, and in My love which is better, by far, than anything you have ever felt. Take time to talk to Me throughout the day, letting Me assure you of My constant attendance.

Someday I will fold you into My arms and hold you until you are satisfied. But for now, rest in the assurance that I am always with you.

Don't ever let go. I am here now.

I will be beside you all day. Think of Me and talk to Me often. I will guide you through whatever happens today.

Wait on Me, beloved.

Trust in Me now.

> *Though you have not seen Him, you love Him; and even*
> *though you do not see Him now, you believe in Him and*
> *are filled with an inexpressible and glorious joy, for you*
> *are receiving the end result of your faith,*
> *the salvation of your souls.*
> *I Peter 1:8-9*

July 17

I will surround you with My love. The knowledge of it will lighten your load.

There are many problems out there, and a lot of pain involved in them. But if you come to Me, I will fill you with love and joy.

Focus on Me, not on your problems.

Let your pain ease and experience the incredible lightness of My being. Hang on to it throughout the day.

I don't want you just to endure this day. I want you to love this day! To be happy in this day!! To spread My love to others in this day!

You can do that with this connection we get in the morning.

If you feel it slipping, find a quiet place again, close your eyes, and envision My presence until you find the joy of My love again.

Oh, there awaits so much joy for you!

For no word from God will ever fail.
Luke 1:37

July 18

$\mathcal{D}$o not let your heart be troubled, dear one. Everything you are facing has been handled by Me.

Trust in Me. Rest in Me.

I would like you to learn how to be more sensitive to My urgings, as it is one of the important ways I seek to communicate with you.

I want to break through the busyness and noise of your daily life and have you in a place where the silence breaks, where you will start being aware of My gentle urgings to guide you.

This will be learned over time. Every day is a baby step towards deeper communion with Me.

Close your eyes and listen. Even in the middle of an urgent situation, I am there with you and if you bow your head in prayer, the Holy Spirit will help guide you through it.

Learning to live in My will enables us to grow closer and closer. It is not a set of commands, it is growth closer to Me where some day you will find unspeakable joy.

So, take a baby step towards real communion with Me today.

Listen . . . listen

Therefore let us move beyond the elementary teachings about Christ and be taken forward to maturity, not laying again the foundation of repentance from acts that lead to death
Hebrews 6:1

July 19

In the early morning light, I await your rising. How I long for you to open your eyes and seek My presence!

If you get up late and rush through the morning without our precious time together, you will miss so much. And so will I.

Just those first few moments of connection will give you the power you need to face the day with My armor on you, and around you, girding you up against evil and sadness.

And I miss you if you don't spend time with me!

Today, do not be afraid of anything you encounter. You have chosen to receive My protection and guidance and all things are possible.

Great things will happen in your life with Me at the helm, even more than you can ever imagine!

Eventually it will become clear.
Eventually you will know.

The Lord is my strength and my shield; my heart trusts in
Him, and He helps me. My heart leaps for joy,
and with my song I praise Him.
Psalm 28:7

July 20

℘isten to Me, beloved. You are precious to Me. I love and adore you.

I have plans for you that you don't know of. Put your trust in Me and I will guide you. You think I am not taking care of you now, but I am.

"Oh, my problems!", you say in your mind. Yes, I know they are there. I will take care of them. Don't worry. I want you to know My mission for you directly.

Trust in Me.
I will direct your path.

Whenever you fear, call out My Name. I am still with you. You are not with Me, but I am with you always. Do not fear or leave the vision I am giving you.

I am with you, even unto the ends of the earth. Know that. Dwell on that.

Abide in Me,
and I will abide in you.

We know also that the Son of God has come and has given us understanding so that we may know Him who is true. And we are in Him Who is true by being in His Son Jesus Christ. He is the true God and eternal life.
I John 5:20

July 21

I will be with you today, dear child. You are the love of My life, and I have always loved and cherished you since you were a baby, before you were born. I will never leave you or forsake you.

Trust in Me.

I will guide you through this day. You know I love you and can feel that I have always been there. There is so much I want to tell you if you will just listen to Me.

Put your hand in Mine. Never let go.

Every day is a new adventure if you follow Me. I will lead you to paths filled with love and light. There is no greater joy than serving Me on this earth.

I made you to love and serve Me. When you do, you will know true happiness because I spend every moment loving and serving you, always watching over you through all the trials and tribulations of this earth.

Every day will be new. Every path will be new. Are you ready? Just hold my hand and together we will climb.

Every day you will climb a little closer to Me.

Surely you have granted him unending blessings and made him glad with the joy of Your presence. For the king trusts in the Lord; through the unfailing love of the Most High he will not be shaken.
Psalm 21:6 - 7

July 22

Just by bringing Me up in your mind often during the day, resting your head with thoughts of Me, I will draw close to you and comfort you. You will learn to sense My presence.

Don't worry about those of the world who question My love and purpose. They have issues only I can handle. They will come to understand one day.

Just focus on your love for Me for I am with you always, even unto the end of the world.

Trust in Me.

I have given you a dream to fulfill for My purpose, that I may be glorified in Christ Jesus. Just follow and I will lead.

Just remember I AM WITH YOU!
Think of Me today, beloved, always.

You will be blessed.

Trust in the Lord with all your heart and lean not on your own understanding; in all your ways submit to Him, and He will make your paths straight.
Proverbs 3:5-6

July 23

In time, My time, all will be fulfilled. Trust in Me.

I want to put My arms around you and take care of you. I am doing that now but you are fighting Me, and you can't feel it or sense it.

Everything happens for a purpose, dear one. In time, we will live together in Heaven. I want you to think about that wonderful reality.

You need to learn to let go and trust Me because I will not let you down. If you think you are alone in this, you are not. You must not give up, because I am guiding you. This is my plan.

I need you to be close to Me. I will direct your pathway. If ever you doubt, you put us back several steps. I want you to depend entirely on Me. I will never let you go.

I don't just feel love, I AM love. Now, go minister to others for Me.

I am with you.

Let the morning bring me word of Your unfailing love, for I have
put my trust in You. Show me the way I should go, for
to You I entrust my life. Rescue me from my enemies,
Lord, for I hide myself in You. Teach me to do
Your will, for You are my God; may Your
good Spirit lead me on level ground.
Psalm 143:8-10

July 24

Think of life as an adventure.

I have plans for you. You are My beloved child.

You may always trust Me because no matter what happens I will always have your best interest at heart.

What is coming up will not be easy but I have promised you that I will always be with you. We will get through this together.

I am not going to tell you what is in your future. Remember, "life is an adventure"? Okay.

Hang on to Me as we fly through the air! Hang on tight because much will be learned that you can share with others.

Today, rest in Me.

I am taking care of things.

> *For I know the plans I have for you," declares the Lord,*
> *"plans to prosper you and not to harm you, plans to*
> *give you hope and a future. Then you will call on Me*
> *and come and pray to Me, and I will listen to you.*
> *Jeremiah 29:11-12*

July 25

I am with you, dear child.

You don't know or understand My purposes for you, but just wait upon Me.

I am answering your prayers, beloved. I know you are scared. Just love and trust Me. I am always with you. In time, you will know all the answers. You see things very differently than I do.

Just trust. Put your hand in Mine. Together we will walk this road. You are always with Me, and I am always with you.

DO NOT BE AFRAID OF THE FUTURE.
I have everything in My hands.

Oh, dear child of Mine, I long to hold you. When you get to heaven, you will sit at my feet and I will tell you stories of others before you. Brave men and women who walked this earth, always by My side. I'm calling you to do that, too, here on earth.

Sometimes it is good to just let go and see where I will take you. A new adventure!

Are you ready? Let go and come along with Me! Letting go totally is the first step. Are you ready? Here we go!

An adventure, beloved. An adventure!

For the Spirit God gave us does not make us timid,
but gives us power, love and self-discipline.
2 Timothy 1:7

July 26

I know you are troubled this morning, dear child. I have My hand on everything in your life. We will take it one step at a time. You may trust fully in Me for the answers. I will take care of you. If there is a time to trust in Me, it is now.

There are powerful enemies all around you, but I have protected you. You will know the answers in time. Right now, it is just important for you to trust Me and to let Me handle it all.

Keep your eyes focused on Me, your heavenly Father. You are not alone in this world. I love you as only a true Father can. Put your hand in Mine and we will walk together through this.

2 Corinthians 1:20 says, "For no matter how many promises I have made, they are "yes" in Christ". That should assure you that the promises I made to My people now include you, as you were officially "adopted" through Christ. I promised over and over to take care of them if they would just love and follow Me.

I have never stopped loving them, or you, My precious child. Put your hand in Mine and we will walk together through this.

You are never alone. I am always with you.

> *For no matter how many promises God has made, they are "Yes" in Christ. And so through Him the "Amen" is spoken by us to the glory of God. Now it is God who makes both us and you stand firm in Christ. He anointed us, set His seal of ownership on us, and put His Spirit in our hearts as a deposit, guaranteeing what is to come.*
> *2 Corinthians 1:20-22*

July 27

Child, I know your pain.

I am with you, now and always, at every step of the way. Whenever you put your foot down, I am walking with you.

Believe in My words, beloved.
I WILL GET YOU THROUGH THIS.

I promise.

You must believe in My promises. I have great things in store for you. Take each day just as it comes. I will raise you up time after time. Only I know how and when.

Keep these words in your heart.

Put your hand in mine and together we will walk through this. Open up your heart and your mind.

Let me guide and direct you.

*Your kingdom is an everlasting kingdom, and Your dominion
endures through all generations. The Lord is trust-
worthy in all He promises and faithful in all He
does. The Lord upholds all who fall and
lifts up all who are bowed down.
Psalm 145:13-14*

July 28

Bless others and I will bless you. Watch and see how I will work. Take one step at a time.

I AM WITH YOU.

Learn to sense My presence. Think of Me as often as you can. Call out to Me. I can hear you.

It is My greatest joy to commune with you.

Go out and face the day with strength. Open your heart and mind to My truth.

My Word is truth.

Let the words of the Bible encourage and guide you. It is My direct message to all who will listen.

Rise up in strength, dear one. Your prayers have been answered. I am with you now and always.

Rest in Me. Trust in Me. You are My most precious child.

Smile, beloved. My peace remains.

Go in My love and peace . . . and smile.

The Lord your God is with you, the Mighty Warrior Who saves. He will take great delight in you; in His love He will no longer rebuke you, but will rejoice over you with singing.
Zephaniah 3:17

July 29

My precious child, I am here. Around you, beside you, in you.

You never need to be afraid. Cast all your cares on Me, because I love you and I will always take care of you.

My peace I give you, My peace I leave with you. In the world you will find no peace, but have joy, for I have overcome the world.

What does that mean to you? It means that every step you take, I am there. I have everything planned for you.

You will not fall. I will catch you.

You wish I would tell you what will happen in your future, but that is not My way. My way is to have you learn to place your trust in Me. If I told you what was going to unfold, you would not grow and learn.

Just trust, dear one. I have said it before over and over. It is the greatest lesson.

Just trust.

In My time you will understand. Go into the day thinking of Me often, calling out to Me. I am with you.

DO NOT BE AFRAID.

> *"Peace I leave with you; My peace I give you. I do not give to you as the world gives. Do not let your hearts be troubled and do not be afraid."*
> *John 14:27*

July 30

I am with you now. I was with you yesterday.

Were you practicing the knowledge of My presence? I would have filled your soul with joy.

Spend time with friends who don't know Me. They need to know of your faith and the peace I give you; the faith and peace I give you to get through all situations.

Let the light of My love fill your words and thoughts. Through this you will receive peace. And you will share that peace with others.

Don't ever be sad, beloved. Count it PURE JOY to endure pain for Me.

Because of sin on this earth, things will never be perfect. But be of good cheer, for I have overcome the world.

I am not making light of your pain. I know it is there. I am saying, "work with it." Use it to better your knowledge of Me, and to share Me.

I am surrounding you right now. My arms wait to hold you securely in My bosom. What joy we will all feel when we are truly together!

Wait on Me. Rest in Me.

Cast your cares on Me, for I am with you.
Here, now, and for always.

> *Cast your cares on the Lord and He will sustain you;*
> *He will never let the righteous be shaken.*
> *Psalm 55:22*

July 31

*R*ise up, My love, and take this day by the hand. It will be a day in which you grow one step closer to Me.

That is all you need.

Whatever loneliness or pain you feel will ease when you spend time with Me. I am the answer to ALL life's situations.

Only enfolded in My loving arms can you find true happiness and release.

Try it now. Close your eyes and envision Me. And know, really know, that I am beside you, loving you and watching over your every step, like a father earnestly watching his toddler.

I am so pleased when you take the right steps, so sad when you wander away from Me.

Because of Jesus' death on the cross, when you return to Me, I am able to forget the pain and sadness I felt, and enfold you into My arms again.

The price for sin has been paid and it is a special day when we start over together!

But you, Sovereign Lord, help me for Your name's sake; out of the goodness of Your love, deliver me. For He stands at the right hand of the needy, to save their lives from those who would condemn them.
Psalm 109:21, 31

August 01

I am near to you now. So close, so real.

Close your eyes and sense My presence.

All your life you have longed for a love that is pure and true. You are starting to sense it as you draw closer to Me through our time together.

Thank you for seeking Me, dear one. For seeking not only to know Me, but to draw into My presence. Our communion together is very precious to Me. You will never regret the time you spend with Me.

Use it throughout the day. Call out My name when you think you can't get through something. When challenges seem overwhelming, tap back into your memory of our time together.

Such peace I will give you, enabling you to soar like an eagle over the highest mountains! You have an attachment to the Almighty that enables you to look down in your flight on all the cares of this world.

I make that possible, beloved one. Only through Me will you find peace through life's hardships.

Hold on now as we soar through the skies!

> *But those who hope in the Lord will renew their strength.*
> *They will soar on wings like eagles; they will run and*
> *not grow weary, they will walk and not be faint.*
> *Isaiah 40:31*

August 02

Put your hand in Mine and place all the worries you are feeling now in it. Let Me take them unto Myself so that your mind may be eased.

I am not only willing, but anxious, to have you cast your cares on Me. I long to help you as a parent longs to help their child.

I see you tossing and turning.
Don't you know yet that I will help?

Letting Me handle your problems is an act of faith, but how you will be rewarded!

How do you do it?

It is as simple as I said. Lay them down at My feet, then take time to stop and listen to the birds. They are singing My praises because they have learned that I will always take care of them.

Reach your hand out.

I am there, My love.
I am there.

Humble yourselves, therefore, under God's mighty hand, that
He may lift you up in due time. Cast all your anxiety
on Him because He cares for you.
I Peter 5:6-7

August 03

Do you know how much I love you? Much more than I could ever express.

I AM LOVE, and it permeates through Me to you.

As you grow to trust in My love, your joy and peace will abound and affect others around you. You will truly be a beacon of My love shining to others in need.

Focus on Me now and throughout the day, stopping to spend precious moments in communion with Me, whether you are at work, at school, or at home.

Anywhere you are, I AM.

David wrote about the closeness of our relationship. If you read through the Psalms, you will be encouraged.

Just as I loved and walked with David, I long to love and walk with you. But do you push Me away by focusing on the distractions or temptations of this evil world?

Come back to Me, dear one. Let Me walk with you and guide you. What could be more easy?

Here I am. Take My hand.

Yet You brought me out of the womb; You made me trust in You, even at my mother's breast. From birth I was cast on You; from my mother's womb you have been my God.
Psalm 22:9-10

August 04

Come to Me this morning, dear child. Let Me wrap My arms around you and comfort you.

The fears you are feeling will melt away when you allow Me to handle them.

Open your eyes today to see all the things I have put in your path. The one I have designed for you will lead to love and happiness. Whether that will be on this side or on the other is for Me to know.

My secret urgings will let you know the way you should go. Trust in them when they come. You will know when they are from Me.

Each day you let Me lead you will also lead us into a closer relationship, one that will be a blessing to you and to others.

"This is what the Lord says, He who made the earth, the Lord who formed it and established it - the Lord is His name: 'Call to me and I will answer you and tell you great and unsearchable things you do not know.'"
Jeremiah 33:2-3

August 05

Come to Me and learn of Me. Treasure our time together as I treasure it.

My Word is full of wonderful stories of love and promises for you to hang onto in your darkest moments. Open it anew every day and let Me enthrall you with the stories from the past.

As near as I was to the Israelites in the Old Testament, I am with you now. As close as Jesus was to the disciples in the New Testament, He is with you now.

You have the assurance of the Rulers of the universe, yet you are scared inside. Where does that come from? It comes from not spending time in My Word.

It is of vital importance in your Christian life.

Armed with verses from scripture, you can slay the dragons that rise up, you can reach out and help a lonely, sick person, and you can give hope to the hopeless.

Most of all, you can rest in the assurance of My love for you and of the sacrifice I made to have this closeness with you.

Don't throw it away, dear one.

Come to Me now.

I gain understanding from Your precepts; therefore I hate
every wrong path. Your word is a lamp for my feet, a
light on my path. I have taken an oath and confirmed
it, that I will follow Your righteous laws.
Psalm 119:104-106

August 06

Today, sensing My presence will be an assurance that I am with you, and that I will take care of you.

Reading stories from the Bible about how I led others will encourage you, dear one, to trust in Me, knowing full well that anything and everything is possible.

Still your soul with that knowledge.

The answer you seek, the provision you ask for, may come in different ways than what you had envisioned. You must trust that I know what you really need far better than you do, and I will provide it.

Like the shepherd out with his flock, guiding and caring for each one of his sheep, I know exactly where I want you to be.

Things might seem murky in your eyes, but not in Mine.
You are where you are now for a purpose.

So just relax in the arms of your Savior and remember the carefree birds who flit about happily knowing that I will always take care of them.

Have mercy on me, my God, have mercy on me, for in You I take refuge. I will take refuge in the shadow of Your wings until the disaster has passed.
Psalm 57:1

August 07

From the recesses of your mind come doubts as to My presence in your life.

Yes, you know I AM, but am I really in your life so completely as I have been saying to you? Do I really love you that much?

Oh, dear one, if you only know how I watch over you continually! I see every step you take, I hear every word you utter, I feel every hurt you feel, and I share with you the times of joy I grant to you.

Do you think that I can share so much with you, yet not love you so completely?

You are made in the image of My Son, so perfectly crafted by My hands. I look at you through eyes of the adoring Father I am. Because of Christ's death for you, I see you as a pure child, wrapped up in innocence and love.

Please do not turn away from Me. Learn to let your insecurities go and accept the security of the extreme love I have for you. Nothing else will matter. I will guide you and take care of you always.

As long as you are in this world, it will take practice. Focus on what I have been telling you.

I am right beside you now, loving you as only I can.

"He himself bore our sins" in His body on the cross, so that we might die to sins and live for righteousness; "by His wounds you have been healed." For "you were like sheep going astray," but now you have returned to the Shepherd and Overseer of your souls.
I Peter 2:24-25

August 08

I will go with you today. I will go with you to the ends of the earth.

Wherever you are, I AM.

I am leading you on a mission for Me. You never need to fear any problems that come up if you are following My lead. I will guide you through them. In fact, it is through these problems that you learn, and grow closer to Me.

I will be with you and will teach you what to say. Just trust in Me. I have already taken care of it. This whole situation is going to be a witness for you to be able to share with others.

Every day will bring new challenges. Rise up to meet them with Me beside you. There should be no fear as we tackle each of them.

My school for you is quite different from earthly schools. And I am the Teacher Who loves you with an everlasting love. My lessons are hard, but the rewards are unimaginable.

I would have you look forward to how we will solve these issues, charging into battle as a mighty warrior with Me at your side!

Today, take a deep breath and know there is nothing we can't handle together.

And relax and smile, for you are deeply loved.

Because He himself suffered when He was tempted,
He is able to help those who are being tempted.
Hebrews 2:18

August 09

Dear child of Mine, today is a new day. One in which the mistakes of yesterday are gone.

If you live closely to Me in My grace, you will be more aware of My presence and I will help you make the right choices.

Every time you stray away from Me, listening instead to the clamor of the world and its desires, you stray farther away from My grace, and loneliness sets into your soul. But sorrow doesn't need to be your friend.

Turn back to Me and joy will fill your life again.

Confused? Just learn to listen to My urgings. Have the abiding peace of My presence in your life, in your everyday decisions. Ultimately, they are steps towards Me or away from Me.

I am not promising you an easy life, but if you stay close to Me, it will be a life of deep joy in My love and salvation, and one day, a life of rewards.

Come to Me now, My child.

The lover of your soul awaits.

You make known to me the path of life; You will fill me
with joy in Your presence, with eternal
pleasures at Your right hand.
Psalm 16:11

August 10

 I love you, precious child of Mine. Always have and always will.

I was anxious to have you be born, to come into this world, because I already knew you, and I wanted to watch you grow in Me.

You took many roads that led you away from Me, even after you found Me. I knew in time that you would come back, and I was watching over you wherever you were.

Rest in My ultimate love, dear one. Nothing will ever compare to it.

Every day is a new adventure if you follow Me. I will lead you to paths filled with love and light. There is no greater joy than serving Me on this earth.

It is why I made you: to love and serve Me.

Then you will know true happiness because I spend every moment loving and serving you, always watching over you through all the trials and tribulations of this earth.

Every day will be new. Every path will be new.
Are you ready? Just hold My hand and together we will climb.

Every day you climb a little closer to Me.

If I rise on the wings of the dawn, if I settle on the far side
of the sea, even there Your hand will guide me,
Your right hand will hold me fast.
Psalm 139:9-10

August 11

From the foundation of the world I had your life planned out, knowing which twists and turns of the road you would choose to travel on.

I have a way prepared for you if you would but learn to take My hand and trust Me to lead you.

I need you to be of strong moral character and stand up against the evil all around you. I want you to take good care of the body I created for you to live in. Your soul is Mine. I have chosen you, redeemed you, and made you Mine.

No more fear. No more second thoughts. We are traveling together and there is so much I have in store for you if you keep on the path with Me. Yes, we will reach the summit, but it will be a much higher one if you stay connected to Me.

I cannot force you to do the things I put in front of you. You must make daily choices for good and evil, for My service, for the personal calling I have for you. If you choose not to follow today, that means we will accomplish a little less.

Please take My hand and let Me lead you into uncharted territory, places you have never been before.

I have so much in store for you if you would but let Me take you there.

In Him we were also chosen, having been predestined
according to the plan of Him who works out everything
in conformity with the purpose of His will, in order that
we, who were the first to put our hope in Christ,
might be for the praise of His glory.
Ephesians 1:11-12

August 12

I am here with you now, beloved, guiding and protecting you.

Never doubt My presence in your life. Focus on it. Dwell in it. It will be a constant source of comfort and strength for you.

Every day you dwell in Me I will guide your path even more. Remember that. I have brought you down to the bottom and now you are listening.

I am here with you now. Listen and grow in Me.

Stay connected. Focus on Me and we will live this life's great adventure!

There are many sheep without a Shepherd in this world. But you are a chosen sheep and I guide, direct and love you.

Do not be hurt if others don't treat you like family. You are My family and that's all that matters. Reach out in love to them for they are lost sheep.

You are My beloved. Act accordingly.

Today, listen to My Holy Spirit and follow His urgings. I am with you, too.

Rest in My love. Have faith in Me.

The Lord is my shepherd, I lack nothing. He makes me lie
down in green pastures, He leads me beside quiet waters,
He refreshes my soul. He guides me along the right
paths for His name's sake.
Psalm 23:1-3

August 13

Every day is a new day, a new beginning. Every sunrise is a new start.

Before you get out of bed in the morning, talk to Me. Devote your day to Me, asking for Me to guide you along the way.

Starting your day this way will bring peace and purpose, knowing that by calling out My name, I will be with you every step.

Call friends who I put in your mind, reminding them of your love for them. Through you they will see and experience My love.

Learn to listen to all My urgings. Be connected to me by hearing the still, quiet voice and then doing what I ask you to. In time you will start hearing it more and more as you grow in Me and learn to trust Me.

Now and forever I am with you, always guiding you, if you will find a quiet place in your soul to listen.

As Jesus was in Me, I am in you.
Rest in that assurance.

All will be fine.

The Lord appeared to us in the past, saying: "I have loved you with an everlasting love; I have drawn you with unfailing kindness."
Jeremiah 31:3

August 14

This morning as you woke up, I put a thought in your head.

Before the TV or music is turned on, before the busyness of your life starts, you are able to hear Me clearer.

Was it about something that went wrong yesterday, or something you did to separate us? Correct it today.

Or was it just a yearning in your soul for closeness to Me? I will grant that, dear one.

My greatest desire is to be as close to you as possible,
for you to lay your head on My chest and to let Me love and care for you.

I am asking you to believe that now.

Close your eyes and envision it, for I am with you, in total love and commitment to our relationship.

Go seek this new day with joy and trust. I will be beside you every moment.

Just close your eyes and know.

Let the beloved of the Lord rest secure in Him, for He shields
Him all day long, and the one the Lord loves
rests between His shoulders.
Deuteronomy 33:12

August 15

How many times I long to comfort you! You don't understand why things are happening the way they are now, and you are scared.

Dear one, I am asking you to trust Me.

What you are going through is a very important time in your life, one during which I am drawing closer to you.

Do you feel Me? I am here with you right now. I will take care of you. I will ease your fears.

As much as it seems to the unbeliever's eye that I have turned from you, I have never been closer. I am here. I will not let you go. Use this time to reach out and touch Me.

Find your quiet place and kneel down and talk to Me. I am with you and very aware of all that is going on. We will walk through this together.

When we get to the other side of this valley, you will be a stronger person. You will not fail. The King of all creation is at your side.

Breathe deeply, and know I am beside you. Rest in the peace of that assurance.

It's ok, dear one. It's okay. I am with you.

> *But if you suffer for doing good and you endure it, this is commendable before God. To this you were called, because Christ suffered for you, leaving you an example, that you should follow in His steps.*
> *I Peter 2:20-21*

August 16

*D*ear child of Mine, you have placed your requests before Me. I will answer them.

I will remember you through all the activities of your day, during times of joy or times of pain. Every thought you have, every step you take, I will know, for I know you.

You are truly with Me, and I with you. Oh, beloved one, you are more in tune with Me than you were before. Your love is opening to me more and more.

Don't you see, if you gave all of yourself, how far we could go together?

I have so many plans for you! You know the path I want you to take. I have given you the vision. The road seems dark, but it is all part of our important journey together, one in which you will grow close to Me.

Don't ever be satisfied with mediocrity. I have a big plan for you. You sense it but are not sure exactly how to get there.

Just come to Me every morning, give your life to Me and together we will start our journey.

What a great day it will be today if you don't let go of My hand!

To humans belong the plans of the heart, but from the Lord comes the proper answer of the tongue. All a person's ways seem pure to them, but motives are weighed by the Lord. Commit to the Lord whatever you do, and He will establish your plans.
Proverbs 16:1-3

August 17

*Y*ou gave your life to Me once. I am asking you to give it anew to Me every morning.

True salvation comes in the daily laying down of your life before Me. Then I can bestow such joy on you, dear one!! Joy that I long to share with you, intimate moments that should never be forgotten.

Write our special moments down. Times when I granted you a miracle, times you felt nearness to Me or received an answer you had been seeking in our times of communion and prayer.

And come to me not only in your mind, but seek Me fervently on your knees, bending low in complete humility, waiting for Me to bestow blessings upon you.

I can never express to you how precious these moments are, and how I long to sweep you up to be with Me in Heaven. But you are here on earth as you must be now, and if you ask Me to, I will never be farther away than a thought.

You are so loved, dear one.

Some day you will know and understand. Until then, just bask in the knowledge by your faith which I have bestowed on you through Jesus Christ.

For our light and momentary troubles are achieving for us an eternal glory that far outweighs them all. So we fix our eyes not on what is seen, but on what is unseen, since what is seen is temporary, but what is unseen is eternal.
2 Corinthians 4:17-18

August 18

Listen to Me this morning, child. You are dear to Me, so very, very precious.

You should face this day with the assurance that you are the child of the King and that you are loved very much.

Whatever trials come up before you today, know that it is the adventure I have set before you, all part of the panorama you will someday watch at My side as we go over your life here on earth.

There will be many scenes that will make you sad because you didn't think of Me and handled things poorly, or perhaps you didn't tell someone who was hurt about Me.

But I am also anxious to have you see the scenes where you did help others unknowingly: just by your presence, by the love you extended, the touch on a lonely person's arm.

I want you to see how your life really makes a difference to so many people here.

Your daily moment-by-moment connection with Me will make you more sensitive to the Holy Spirit's urgings towards those around you in need.

Walk with me today, dear one.
Make memories you will want to watch one day with Me.

For now we see only a reflection as in a mirror; then we
shall see face to face. Now I know in part; then I shall
know fully, even as I am fully known.
I Corinthians 13:12

August 19

Out of the recesses of your mind come thoughts that make you wonder where they came from. A momentary guilt washes over you as you correct them.

Where did they come from, you ask? They come from the evil one himself, the one cast out of heaven so long ago. He parades this earth hoping to take captive those who do not ally themselves with Me. Those he captures are not just the weak ones. They are strong leaders of nations, of large corporations, all the way down to the lonely person on the street.

Your connection with Me enables you to push those evil thoughts (and satan himself!) right out of your mind. As time goes on, he will try harder and harder to collect those nearest to Me.

Stay close, dear one, for with Me you will have protection and love. Remember I have already defeated him, and he is just desperate to have as many people as possible go with him through the gates of hell. You have all the power you need to overcome whatever he puts in front of you. He is very real, dear one.

Don't ever let go of our connection.
Keep your eyes on Me and you will find true joy!

Every spirit that does not acknowledge Jesus is not from God. This is the spirit of the antichrist, which you have heard is coming and even now is already in the world. You, dear children, are from God and have overcome them, because the One who is in you is greater than the one who is in the world.
I John 4:3-4

August 20

Lift your eyes up to Me this morning, for there you will find the peace you so fervently seek. You will not find it in worldly pleasures.

Look up. Seek My presence in your life.

I know everything that is going on. I know each of your issues. The answers haven't come yet, and you wonder if I even know or care.

Oh, I do, dear one. I know things you don't and because of that, I am asking you to trust Me.

When all the world seems bleak, when you don't think you can go on any further, you can, for I am with you, and all will work out in My time.

I am your Shepherd, guiding you constantly if you let Me.

Just look up and trust Me.

The Lord is a refuge for the oppressed, a stronghold in times of trouble. Those who know Your name will trust in You, for You, Lord, have never forsaken those who seek You.
Psalm 9:9-10

August 21

Come deep with Me, My love. Walk with Me through gardens of time.

Sense Me. Feel Me.

I am all around you.

Learn to draw Me into yourself so that there I may abide with you through all of life's challenges. The joy you will find is incomparable.

Come walk with Me, beloved, deeply, earnestly seeking My presence.

You will find me.

A storehouse of love and joy awaits.

Deep calls to deep in the roar of Your waterfalls; all Your
waves and breakers have swept over me. By day the
Lord directs His love, at night His song is with me.
Psalm 42:7-8

August 22

I love you fully, dear child. Fully and completely.

Learning to let go and let Me show you My love is one of the most wonderful gifts I can give you.

Practice it now. Close your eyes and think of Me. Consciously put all the activities of your day in My hands. Release it entirely to Me.

Trust that I am with you and that I will guide you through everything.

The peace that you feel when you free yourself of your problems and allow Me to take them over is My gift to you. We have grown one step closer on our journey together.

How precious that is to Me!
How precious you are to Me!

Hold My hand tightly, beloved, for I am at the helm of your life. Don't ever let go.

Smooth sailing? No, but come and experience the connection. You will never go back.

I love you, dear one.

And the peace of God, which transcends all understanding,
will guard your hearts and your minds in Christ Jesus.
Philippians 4:7

August 23

Thank you, child, for the profession of your love for Me. I love to hear you say it.

Only I am Love, but I know your love, and it is beautiful for Me to hear you profess it.

Don't be afraid, dear one, for I am with you.

The problems you are swimming in are not insurmountable. I know they are there, and I am taking care of them in My time.

Your job is to trust Me and to never doubt Me.

Look up to Me with your soul. Seek My presence with your whole heart and you will find Me. I will never let you down.

Don't be weary. Come to Me and I will give you rest.

You are Mine, beloved: the personal and adored creation of My hands.

Have joy in this knowledge!

"You will seek Me and find Me when you
seek Me with all your heart."
Jeremiah 29:13

August 24

Precious child of Mine, let Me draw you into My presence now. Close your eyes and think of Me.

I am truly with you now.

Don't worry about the problems you face today. I have already handled them. You need only to put one foot in front of the other and hold My hand.

Together we can do anything!!

Have you anything in your life that requires washing? Cleansing from your soul?

Search your heart, My child. Make it clean.

Come to Me unburdened by the sin of this world so that I may bestow blessings upon you.

You are Mine, dear one. I have chosen you.

Come and find peace in Me.

Search me, God, and know my heart; test me and know my anxious thoughts. See if there is any offensive way in me, and lead me in the way everlasting.
Psalm 139:23-24

August 25

To see Me fully, you must give yourself fully. Fully and completely.

I do not ask too much, dear one. The rewards you will receive will be beyond your greatest imagination.

In this world, you have a conception of what and who you think I am. Your study of works by men and woman who have known and loved Me will not fully explain what I can be to you.

The love I have for you is also not something that can be fully explained on paper, or something you think you understand because you have felt love for someone else. My love for you alone is larger than life, more than you can begin to conceive. Receive it today, beloved.

Let Me enfold you into My arms to love you, hold you and take care of you fully. Through this surrender on your part, you will begin to learn about Me personally. Through time and constant surrender, you will see what I can do in your life.

Someday we might write a book about it so others may be inspired, but words become weak in light of My love.

You will come to know Who I AM by your relationship with Me.

You and Me. Me and you.

Accept it today, beloved. The Lover of your soul awaits.

For now we see only a reflection as in a mirror; then we
shall see face to face. Now I know in part; then I
shall know fully, even as I am fully known.
1 Corinthians 13:12

August 26

Stop counting up all your problems in your head. No good will come from that. On the other side of your problems, you can praise Me, for I have handled them for you.

You will see the miracles in them.

The harder the problem, the greater the victory, the more I can be glorified.

Our story will help others to find Me. Isn't that what this life is about?

I want others to see Me in you, dear one. Stay close and listen, for I am always ready to make our story come alive.

Walking with Me daily is the greatest joy of this earth. You will find peace, dear one, no matter how insurmountable your problems seem.

Bring them all to Me.
A new story is waiting to unfold.

The righteous cry out, and the Lord hears them;
He delivers them from all their troubles.
Psalm 34:17

August 27

You are still so overwhelmed with your problems. Don't you know by laying them at My feet that I will take care of them?

You need only to trust Me.

You will receive peace and joy and be able to thank Me because we have grown closer, and I have been glorified just in the release of all the problems you carry with you.

I understand how hard it is for you to lay them at My feet. If only you would understand how rewarding it will be! Why do you want to shoulder it all when the Ruler of all wants to take care of them and of you?

Put your hand in Mine, dear one.
Close your eyes and breathe My love in deeply.

Trust Me.

It takes trust to know I am with you. But time together will increase your faith. You will come to know, really know, that I am beside you, longing for closeness with you.

I am here, dear one.
Just let go and trust Me.

The Lord is a refuge for the oppressed, a stronghold in times of trouble. Those who know Your name trust in You, for You, Lord, have never forsaken those who seek You.
Psalm 9:9-10

August 28

Child, you are in My care.

Your heart is seeking Me, and I am so glad. Our time together in the morning is very precious to Me.

Wear Me throughout the day. Don My protective armor and shield to face whatever comes your way.

I am in you and around you. Together we can do anything!

Every step you take with Me I have planned for you. The steps you take away from Me, I make good out of when you come back.

But how sad that makes Me to see you reject not only Me, but the sacrifice We made for you on the cross!

Nothing will compare, dear one.

The price has been paid, but new wounds are made when you reject that gift. Every time you reject the Holy Spirit's urgings, you take one step away.

Learn to listen and obey. I am the still, small voice. The more you listen and obey, the more I will lead you.

Continue lifting your heart towards Me this day.
There will be so much joy!!

The night is nearly over; the day is almost here. So, let us put
aside the deeds of darkness and put on the armor of light.
Romans 13:12

August 29

Entwine your soul with Mine. Lift yourself above the world and float through time and space with Me.

I am with you, beloved. I have so much love for you. Let Me carry you. You are bearing many burdens that I long to help you with.

You can find joy in anything.

What kind of statement is that, you ask? How can there be joy in pain and hardship?

The joy will be found in Me: In knowing My plan for your life; in trusting Me no matter what; in giving Me your utmost pain; in letting go, releasing the pain and weight that you bear.

Come to Me now and let it go. Fall into My arms and let Me hold you close. Soon I can tell you face to face why. One day it will all be over. I feel the pain you feel and I will always take care of you.

Come with Me now. Close your eyes, dear one.
Imagine My presence. I am so close.

Lay your head on My chest.
I am with you now.

And the God of all grace, who called you to His eternal glory
in Christ, after you have suffered a little while, will himself
restore you and make you strong, firm and steadfast.
To Him be the power for ever and ever.
I Peter 5:10-11

August 30

Why is your heart so heavy this morning, child? Don't you know that I, the Lord, dwell in you? Take control of your emotions. Think of Me. Know that I am with you. Let Me give you My joy and peace.

In the world there are many troubles. You are no longer of this world. The day you accepted Me you became a future resident of Heaven. You are only here for a season.

Make it a season of learning how to grow closer to Me, studying the Word so that you know of My personality, the struggles that Jesus endured on earth, and the love We have for you.

Learn how to really commune with Me. Bring your requests and your thanks to Me often during the day and know that I am, oh, so close to you always.

I see every tear, I hear every word spoken in love or anger. I know every painful, injurious thought in your mind.

It is all Mine, beloved, for you are Mine.

Come find the joy I bring. Let Me carry the load for you. No, let Me carry you and the load!!

Smile, for you are loved.

> *The Lord is close to the brokenhearted and saves those who*
> *are crushed in spirit. The righteous person may have*
> *many troubles, but the Lord delivers him from them all.*
> *Psalm 34:18-19*

August 31

*O*h, how beautiful the morning of your soul! The sweet urgings of My presence that come to you when you first wake up.

Listen to them, dear one.

Talk to Me before you get out of bed. Give your day over to Me, your plans over to Me, so that we will face each and every challenge together in My perfect plan.

What is the perfect plan?
Your daily walk with Me, letting Me lead you through life.

Living in My will will lead to joy you have not felt before: the joy of perfect love surrounding you always.

Yes, you will slip, but I will be there to catch you. I am always near.

Face today with courage, dear one.
I have so much in store for you!!

In their hearts humans plan their course,
but the Lord establishes their steps.
Proverbs 16:9

September 01

*A*re you Mine?

Have you heard My voice? Yes, because you are learning how to listen.

I have always been close, desiring this nearness to you, but you have not tried to hear Me.

Perhaps it wasn't as possible because the television or loud music was constantly blaring, or you were consumed with worry about your circumstances.

Come away to Me, beloved. Come to the still quietness of My presence. Sit at My feet and learn of Me.

I love you with an everlasting love. That means I loved you before the foundation of the world, before you were born, throughout all your life, and even after you die.

I hold you in the palm of My hand with such love!

You are Mine, blessed one. I have chosen you.

Take My hand.

Come to Me and learn of Me.

This is what the Sovereign Lord, the Holy One of Israel,
says: "In repentance and rest is your salvation, in
quietness and trust is your strength."
Isaiah 30:15

September 02

℘very day is a new beginning. Seize it with joy in Me. Learn to be aware of the beauty all around you.

I am in that beauty. I give it to you as a reminder of My presence, as a proof of My reality.

Such care I took with each creature created in the colors, shape, the inner workings of each and every one of them. They are a gift from Me to you.

Seek them out. Take time out of your busy schedule to go out in nature. Sit quietly and notice them, large and small, butterflies to horses, caterpillars to elephants.

They are all My creation,

but My crowning glory was you.

How intricate and perfect I made your body to be! You are so beautiful in My sight! And so deeply loved!

My heart overflows when you choose to spend time with Me.

Face this day knowing you are a child of the King; not just born into this chaotic, evil world, but lovingly formed into the person I created you to be, one of whom I am very proud.

"Father, I want those you have given Me to be with Me where
I am, and to see My glory, the glory you have given Me
because you loved Me before the creation of the world."
John 17:24

September 03

℘lose your eyes and dream of Me. Let Me take you to faraway places where just you and I abide.

Imagine Jesus' resurrection from the grave. What inexpressible joy there was! Like no other ever!

Those days without Him were the darkest days ever. Yet, when He arose from the tomb, so full of triumph, how we all rejoiced!!

The greatest sacrifice ever to be made was over! The separation from My Beloved Son was ended! If only you could have seen Him kneeling at My feet when He returned!

What love was poured out by Him and I for you!

Do not reject it, dear one. He withstood all glory and comfort to die a horrible death, separated from Me to atone for your sin.

And I endured the horrible pain of knowing I could prevent My Son from this pain and abandonment.

Yet for you, I did nothing but watch.

Talk to Him now, thanking Him for this ultimate gift. Think of it often in prayer, remembering, and let it help you to understand even just a little of the love We have for you.

Just as people are destined to die once, and after that to face judgment, so Christ was sacrificed once to take away the sins of many; and He will appear a second time, not to bear sin, but to bring salvation to those who are waiting for Him.
Hebrews 9:27-28

September 04

Oh, My child, you are here with Me now, restoring your soul, finding strength and joy in our communion.

There is so much I want to share with you.
So much I want you to learn.

Come and see that I am good, that I love you more than anything you can ever imagine.

Feel the joy of completeness in Me, for in that you will have true peace and happiness.

I am never farther away than the whisper of My name. At your slightest cry all heaven can come to your aid.

There is power in our connection, beloved.
Use it for good. Use it for faith.

And know, really, really know that I am here now beside you, guiding you.

Just ask.

Therefore confess your sins to each other and pray for each other so that you may be healed. The prayer of a righteous person is powerful and effective.
James 5:16

September 05

*E*ach day that you awake from sleep is a new start. How creation sings My praise in the morning as the sun creeps up over the horizon! Every living creature knows of Me and thanks Me for their very existence.

Do you? Don't be so busy that you fail to spend that precious morning time with Me. It will determine the outcome of your day. Look forward to it.

I watch over you in the night, and I watch over you when you are awake. I would be so happy if your first thoughts were of Me, talking to Me, asking Me to continue keeping you and your family safe during the day, guiding you, helping you to make the right decisions, helping you to say the right words in moments of stress.

You can have this lifeline to Me if you just ask for it.

I want this type of relationship with you so much that I sent My Son to die alone on a cross.

Words can't describe it, but don't you see?

The Lover of your soul awaits, dear one. Just ask.

I long to hear your words to Me in the morning, or at any time.

Come home to My love. Come home to peace.
Just spend time with Me.

> *"I am with you and will watch over you wherever you go,*
> *and I will bring you back to this land. I will not leave*
> *you until I have done what I have promised you."*
> *Genesis 28:15*

September 06

Oh, dear child of Mine, you are feeling lost today. Not from me, but from the situations in this world. Do not let them overwhelm you.

One day you will understand why everything has happened the way it has. Some people make choices apart from Me with disastrous consequences. Others have given their lives to Me and you don't understand why I don't make their life easy.

Please trust Me, dear one. I know the best.

When you come to understand, you will concur that all My decisions brought good.

Through pain, through loss, through hardship, I WAS ALWAYS THERE.

I will never leave your side, for you are the love of My life for whom My heart sings.

Trust Me.

Sow righteousness for yourselves, reap the fruit of unfailing
love, and break up your unplowed ground; for it is time
to seek the Lord, until He comes and showers
His righteousness on you.
Hosea 10:12

September 07

Come to Me, you who are heavy-laden, and I will give you rest.

How many times have you heard that, yet they were just words in your ear?

The joy I feel when you come to Me is indescribable.

I see you so worried, so upset. Yet, all you need to do is come to Me and lay your burdens and yourself at My feet and I will carry the load for you.

I will pick you up in My arms and carry you to a place where you will feel safe and warm.

Resting in My arms, all your cares will melt away.

Come to Me now, dear one.
I am always waiting, always near.

"Come to me, all you who are weary and burdened,
and I will give you rest."
Matthew 11:28

September 08

Travel the world today wrapped in My light. Face the daily situations with total abandon of the pressure and stress you are feeling, for you are My child, the child of the King of all.

What possibly could you fear when all heaven is at your side? You have the armor of righteousness and salvation.

Look for others in need who don't know about Me and My love for them. Let them know how they, too, can have the joy of this assurance.

And in the evening, come home and rest yourself. Bathe in the light of My presence and sleep the sleep of a baby who knows his every need will be fulfilled.

How I love you, dear chosen one of Mine!!
The earth is at your feet, for I conquered it long ago.

Travel with Me now through the day.
I will be beside you all the way.

Finally, be strong in the Lord and
in His mighty power.
Ephesians 6:10

September 09

How I long to gather My children unto Me, as a mother hen gathers her little chicks, to protect them from the evil one, and make their path happy and safe!

Come to Me in the freshness of the morning. I await you and look forward to this time together every day.

Where is your mind now? Is it struggling to concentrate on learning of Me?

As much as it hurts Me, I chose to give everyone free will, and the devil has made this morning connection with Me difficult because he knows its vital importance. He does it through making your days packed with busyness, and when you do come to Me, he makes it seem boring compared to the enticements of the world.

But there is nothing more precious and nothing more important than connecting with Me at the beginning of your day. When you do, I arm you with strength to face the day, and with power over the enemy who constantly tries to sever our connection. He knows how strong it can be, and it threatens him. He has absolutely no power where I am asked to be involved.

Come to Me, child.

Let Me gather you under My wings here you will find peace and strength.

> *"Jerusalem, Jerusalem, you who kill the prophets and stone those sent to you, how often I have longed to gather your children together, as a hen gathers her chicks under her wings, and you were not willing."*
> *Luke 13:34*

September 10

Dear child of Mine, you are confused and worried today. Don't you know to let Me carry your load?

I stand waiting, ready to help you.

I have everything in My hands: you, all of your problems, all the good you have ever done, all the mistakes you have made.

Let Me take care of you and I will make everything work out for good.

Where are you in the vision I have given you?

Do you steadfastly work towards that goal? Never doubt that together we can accomplish it.

I will never let you down, dear one.

Take My hand.

And we know that in all things God works for the good
of those who love Him, who have been called
according to His purpose.
Romans 8:28

September 11

Let Me fill your life with joy this morning, beloved one!

True, unadulterated joy.

The joy of knowing you are loved and protected by the Ruler of the universe Who so lovingly planned and created you.

I can fill your soul to the brim with My peace and love. I can soothe your soul, aching though it may be, with tenderness and mercy. I can give you hope again for the future.

I can gather you into My arms and hold you until your fears subside and I can tell you the truths from My Word that will encourage you and give you purpose.

"Yes," you say, "I want all of those things!"

They are there but for the taking, dear one. I long to grant you this and so much more!

Just ask. Just trust. Just believe.

You can't be more loved than you are right now. Reach out your hand. Let Me take it in Mine.

You are OK now for you are with Me.

You are loved so very, very much.

He will yet fill your mouth with laughter
and your lips with shouts of joy.
Job 8:21

September 12

How beautiful are the feet of those who toil for Me! I will guide their steps until we are together. I will show them the path to peace and love.

It is only found in Me, dear one. Only in Me.

There are many people who seem to have it all, but they do not. They ache inside. They want the true meaning of life. They lie awake in the middle of the night, frightened. And in the morning, they continue on in their meaningless lives, striving more and more fervently for money, power and fame.

But I have chosen you, and you are walking with Me. Your greatest success will not be on this earth. It is on the other side with Me.

So do not envy those who seem to have no problems. Their deepest souls are frightened.

Those who love and serve Me are filled with joy and peace through the knowledge of My love for them through Jesus Christ, My only begotten Son.

Keep your eyes fixed on Me, beloved.
You have chosen to walk with Me.

Only on this path is there true joy.

> *"You are my witnesses," declares the Lord, "and my servant whom I have chosen, so that you may know and believe Me and understand that I am He. Before Me no god was formed, nor will there be one after Me. I, even I, am the Lord, and apart from Me there is no savior."*
> *Isaiah 43:10-11*

September 13

How I have longed for the closeness you desire! It is a positive step that you, too, are feeling this desire to be close to Me.

The best way to do that is to simply trust. Trust in Me. Trust in My presence.

Know that I am beside you, loving you, all the way.

In this life you will have trouble. My desire is not to take you away from those troubles, but through those troubles, to draw you into Myself.

You will grow so much!!

Every decision you make determines our relationship. If you follow the Holy Spirit's urging, you are drawing one step closer to Me.

Every time you ignore the urgings, I have to step back a little. Not from loving and caring for you, but from a deeper communion with you.

Open the door, beloved, and let the floodgates of My love and joy fill you up.

"I have told you these things, so that in Me you may have peace. In this world you will have trouble. But take heart! I have overcome the world."
John 16:33

September 14

Surround yourself today with the peace of My presence. Let it invade your very soul. Breathe it in deeply and exhale all the cares of this world.

How will you know, absolutely know, I am with you?
By your breathing.

I give you life, dear one. I created you in your mother's womb. I formed your fingers and toes, your eyes and hair, and made your heart beat.

When you were born, I had you draw your first breath of air into the lungs I so lovingly designed.

I am the Creator.
You are My masterpiece.

Go through the day with that assurance. Consciously breathe in My love and presence and breathe out the pain and loneliness.

I still know every beat of your heart. I am with you now in this way.

Soon you will see Me face-to-face. What a glorious day that will be!

Know, beloved. Really know!

For You created my inmost being; You knit me together in my mother's womb. I praise You because I am fearfully and wonderfully made. Your works are wonderful, I know that full well.
Psalm 139:13-14

September 15

*D*o I remember you? Yes, beloved.

I remember you now and always. You are in My thoughts every moment of your day.

Always.

Just when you think something disastrous is going to happen, it all turns out ok. Your understanding of the word disastrous is redefined, because with Me you can go through anything. I will never allow it to happen if I know you cannot handle it.

Know that it is always in My hands. Don't be angry at Me if it doesn't go the way you planned, or if it didn't go the way you think it needed to.

There is so much you don't understand now, but one day you will.

Even if something bad happened because you strayed from Me, when you return to the safety of My arms, I will make it all turn out okay.

That's how much I love you!!

I watch over your every move. Trust in Me for the outcomes.

I will always take care of you.

Yet I will remember the covenant I made with you in the
days of your youth, and I will establish an
everlasting covenant with you.
Ezekiel 16:60

September 16

*Y*our heart is filled with gratitude this morning as you learn more about Me.

I love your thanks and praise not just for Me, but because it is good for you.

When you praise Me, it lightens your soul. It promotes health and frees your spirit. Always find time every day to thank Me for the blessings I have bestowed upon you.

Go to your quiet place and make a list of the things you can think of that I have blessed you with. Refer to these every day and write more down as I enlighten you.

Doing this simple practice will help you be aware of how closely I watch over you. You will become more sensitive to it when even little things happen.

My hand is working in your life, all part of your pathway towards Me, dear one.

Come, sit at My knee and let Me share My love with you!

So then, just as you received Christ Jesus as Lord, continue
to live your lives in Him, rooted and built up in Him,
strengthened in the faith as you were taught,
and overflowing with thankfulness.
Colossians 2:6-7

September 17

Child of Mine, as the morning breaks over the mountains, I am thinking of you.

You are in My mind now and always. Even when you were asleep, I was watching you. Every moment that goes by I completely surround you with My love and care.

I want you to remember that today when your problems seem overwhelming, and it seems you can't breathe. Remember Me and My love for you, and how we can walk through, over, under and around anything that comes up.

I am your strength.

Did you know you have your own angel? He is also with you. You are well taken care of, beloved.

Never fear. I will never let you down.

I am not just helping you through situations on earth, I am guiding you to bigger and better places. The plans I have for you are greater than you can imagine.

I just need you to trust Me and to walk with Me.
Together we will reach the stars.

For He will command His angels concerning you to guard
you in all your ways; they will lift you up in their hands,
so that you will not strike your foot against a stone.
Psalm 91:11-12

September 18

How precious you are to Me, dear one! I look at you with such pride and love.

How with pride, you ask? When you accepted Me and My love through Christ's death on the cross, and asked forgiveness for your sins, I covered you with His blood. And when I look at you now, I see a pure child, a child whose purity is as white as snow.

So, when you come to Me, come with the security of knowing that you are no longer covered in sin, even though you may have sinned terribly the day before. When you ask forgiveness for that sin, I throw it away, down deep into the sea, and My lamb remains pure.

Because of Jesus' sacrifice, there are no barriers between us. No past problems, no past sins.

I see your face and I long to cup it in My hands and tell you how much your Father loves you.

Believe that, dear one.
Know it from the bottom of your heart.

You and Me. Me and you.

"Come now, let us settle the matter," says the Lord.
"Though your sins are like scarlet, they shall be as
white as snow; though they are red as
crimson, they shall be like wool."
Isaiah 1:18

September 19

Listen to the cheerful calls of the birds this morning as they sing My praises. You can hear them chatter and trill through the early morning hours. Although they continue through the day, their sounds of praise are muffled by the sounds of the busy world.

Find time to come apart from that world and listen again. Rest your soul by clearing your mind of your problems and focus on Me.

Train yourself to listen to the silence. Is the wind blowing through the trees? Are the leaves rustling? Can you hear the locusts? Can you hear the birds?

Are you in a busy city where it is hard to hear? Close your eyes and remember when you were in a place where you were able to. Let the memory of the sounds come alive in your mind.

Although I am beside you wherever you are, nature is in constant praise of Me, and you will sense My presence more when you surround yourself either in nature, or in the memory of it. Finding this quiet place and time will arm your soul with peace: a very important shield in your world.

Finally, dear one, do not let the clamors of the world overwhelm you. You are a child of the King.

Face this day with the knowledge of My love.

For since the creation of the world God's invisible qualities -
His eternal power and divine nature - have been clearly
seen, being understood from what has been made,
so that people are without excuse.
Romans 1:20

September 20

I have given you power, dear one, in the Name of My Son, Jesus, to conquer all the evil in this world.

Power to heal and to help.
Power to love and to let go.

Do you use it? Do you call on that power? As My child, it is your birthright. Use it to glorify Me.

By helping others, I am glorified.
By standing strong against the evil one, I am glorified.

Together we can face anything, dear one. You will always be victorious if I am with you.

Take My hand and feel the power that I offer to you. Never go without it.

Let Me protect you, guide you and keep you in My love, now and always.

I pray that the eyes of your heart may be enlightened in order that you may know the hope to which He has called you, the riches of His glorious inheritance in His holy people, and His incomparably great power for us who believe.
Ephesians 1:18-19

September 21

*A*re you sad this morning? Do your troubles seem overwhelming?

They are not. Nothing is, when you stay connected to Me, allowing Me to help you.

There IS an answer. There is ALWAYS hope.

Never let yourself give up on the dream or passion I gave you. And never give up on the person for whom you have been praying.

There is an answer, dear one.

Perhaps not the easy answer you are seeking, but as your love entwines itself now with Mine, you will learn to wait patiently for My timing and My answers.

For I love you more than you love yourself.

I love the one you are praying for more than you can.

So, trust in Me, beloved. You have chosen Me, and I will work everything out for the best.

Trust in that knowledge.

Be joyful in hope, patient in affliction, faithful in prayer.
Romans 12:12

September 22

*O*h, how the heavens are available to help you each and every day!!

What does that mean? All heaven stands ready to come to your aid if you but ask.

Call in the troops! Bring your requests to Us. Nothing is too big or too small for Us.

I want to have this power displayed on earth, but few today sincerely ask for it and believe that it is possible.

The Bible is full of stories of men and women who believed in Me and acted on it. I was with them, just as I am with you.

I have a mission for you to fulfill. It may be right in your backyard, or it may be in a faraway country. You know, or are discovering, the plan I have for you.

Don't ever give up, no matter your age. I will not be done working in you and through you until your dying breath!

What joy as you reach up to the stars in our quest!

You see, I have great joy as well, for I will be beside you all the way, urging you on, slowly unveiling the fullness of My dream to you each step you take in faith.

I am so pleased with you, My child. Believe that, and trust in Me.

Do not be anxious about anything, but in every situation,
by prayer and petition, with thanksgiving,
present your requests to God.
Philippians 4:6

September 23

Close your eyes and envision My presence. Let Me enfold you into My loving arms where you will find true peace and joy.

Don't search for these gifts in the world. You will not find them there.

Today, I am asking you to take a step of faith. To step out towards the vision I am giving you. Don't falter or look down.

Your strength and direction come from on high.

You are not alone on this journey, for I am ever with you. Whatever obstacles rise up before you can be conquered through Me.

I have given you a purpose for your life, dear one. It is a high calling. Don't be overwhelmed by it.

If I chose to show you the end from the beginning, and you continue to follow Me, you would be astounded at where I led you. But if you followed the way of the world, the sight you see will be sad indeed.

Someday we will look at your life together.

Take My hand, dear one. Let Me take you into uncharted territory, to the most intimate walk with Me.

Let your legacy be: "You walked with God."

He has showed you, O mortal, what is good. And what does
the Lord require of you? To act justly and to love
mercy and to walk humbly with your God.
Micah 6:8

September 24

Ever wonder where a butterfly comes from, or how there are so many different ones with brilliant patterns and colors splashed on their wings?

We had fun creating them, hoping you would take time to notice and appreciate their unusual beauty.

So much of creation is a reminder of Who I am, and how much I love you.

Have you ever noticed the spots on a jaguar, the brilliant colors of tropical fish? The earth is teeming with creatures too beautiful to have "evolved!"

They were created for you, to bring your mind to Me. Even if someone never has the ability to get close to a Bible, they can find Me through nature.

Take time to study it. Go to places where you can experience it firsthand. When you do, you are drawing out of the busyness of the world and taking time to refresh your love and gratitude for Me.

Nature sings praises to Me all the time. Join them in their festive songs and draw ever closer to the Lover of your soul.

For since the creation of the world God's invisible qualities-
His eternal power and divine nature-have been clearly
seen, being understood from what has been made,
so that people are without excuse.
Romans 1:20

September 25

This morning I was watching you as you slept. I saw you wake up and longed to reach out and gather you into My arms as a father would, to comfort and care for his beloved child. But I resisted and let you arise to start your day.

Did you start it with Me?
Did you ask for My presence to fill you with strength and courage?

How you start the day is crucial, dear one. Gaining access to Me is always available for you, but those first waking moments set a standard for the whole day. Once we have made the connection, I can fill you with My love, joy and purpose.

We have a purpose, dear one. A noble purpose! One in which you walk with Me side by side, reaching out to help those in need, touching the shoulder of one in pain, encouraging those around you. Through our connection, I will make you aware of them.

So many are hurting, in need of the knowledge of My love and care for them.

That is your purpose today, dear child.

Listen to My gentle urgings.
You will see and know.

Let the morning bring me word of Your unfailing love, for
I have put my trust in You. Show me the way I
should go, for to You I entrust my life.
Psalm 143:8

September 26

I will guide you through the confusing issues of today, and tomorrow, and to the end of the world.

You are My beloved one and I will not let confusion separate us.

When you spend time with Me, I will cause confusing things to become clear. Nothing will stand between us if you come to Me with an open mind.

Obey Me.

Walk the path I have given you and I will never let you down. You are never farther away from Me than a thought or a whispered prayer.

So, do not be troubled about the future, for I am always with you, guiding and protecting you.

Take My hand and we will walk through all problems and all confusing situations.

But from everlasting to everlasting the Lord's love is with those who fear Him, and His righteousness with their children's children, with those who keep His covenant and remember to obey His precepts.
Psalm 103:17-18

September 27

*Y*ou bring your requests to Me in Jesus' name. Do you know how precious that is to Me?

My very existence is tied to love for My beloved Son. I want Him to be worshipped and glorified.

He has always been with Me. We knew even before Eve took the first bite of the forbidden apple that Jesus would have to go down to earth. There was a part of us that wanted Him to go and experience everything through the eyes of the humans We had created.

But there was a larger part of Us that dreaded the horrible pain He would go through, the rejection; total humiliation from those We created and loved. And then the awful separation as I withdrew and let Him die, so alone and in so much pain, bearing the weight of the world's sin on His beautiful shoulders.

So, when you come to Me in prayer and close the prayer, "In Jesus' Name", a thousand electric bolts go through the air as what you have said has special significance or special delivery.

"In Jesus' Name" . . . how precious to hear. How wonderful that you, My beloved, chosen child, would come to Me in the Name of the Most precious Being in the universe "In Jesus' Name." I have afforded that statement all the power in the world. And to you, My child, I have given that power, through Jesus in Jesus' Name.

"You did not choose me, but I chose you and appointed you that you might go and bear fruit - fruit that will last - and so that whatever you ask in My name, the Father will give you."
John 15:16

September 28

Child, the road I am asking you to walk with Me on is only for you. Don't look at others' walk. I have created you and prepared you for this time.

Do not think you are walking alone, for I am always beside you.

Not only have I given you this vision, I have equipped you for it. You have every tool you need to march forward.

Don't be discouraged when the way looks impossible. Absolutely NOTHING is impossible with Me. You will fulfill that vision if you take My hand.

I will never forsake you or let you down.

He Who loves you more than you can ever understand is right beside you, equipping you.

Take My hand, beloved one.

For this God is our God for ever and ever;
He will be our guide even to the end.
Psalm 48:14

September 29

*H*ow precious you are to Me, dear child! How I love our time together!

Did I awaken you this morning and encourage you to spend this time with Me? I want to draw so close to you, but the only way you can learn of Me is by choosing to spend this time with Me.

Don't get drawn in by the distractions of the world. That is why I ask you to come to Me first thing, before your day starts.

satan is very intimidated by our time together. If you wait and try to fit it in later, he will see to it that your day is way too busy. He knows that when you come to Me, I will give you My shield of protection covering you with love, and that it will help you to listen and obey Me, and to think of Me throughout the day.

Our morning time together gives you the strength to face anything he throws at you.

Come and let Me draw you into My arms, dear one. Let Me surround you with My love. Lay your head upon My chest. Close your eyes and know I am here, and I am real, and know that there is no other love like this anywhere on this earth.

Go out into the day now, armed with My presence.

Abide in My love and joy.

Let the morning bring me word of Your unfailing love, for
I have put my trust in You. Show me the way I
should go, for to You I entrust my life.
Psalm 143:8

September 30

*L*et Me fill your soul this morning with the good news of salvation!

Yes, you have heard it before. The day is drawing near when I will welcome you into Heaven with Me. The whole earth was created to accomplish this purpose, to show how good triumphs over evil. And soon Jesus will come again to draw you up to Me so we can rejoice together!

How I long for that day!
For the pain and suffering in this world to stop!
For all My chosen ones to see Me face to face!

What joy there will be throughout the kingdom! All the preparations here have been made and we are waiting until the chosen day when it will all be over.

Until that time, when Jesus returns, or until I call you home privately, draw near to Me. Learn to listen to My urgings. Let Me keep you close and guide you safely through your time here.

I can't help but be heartened, beloved, for our time is near.

Be joyful today in the knowledge of your salvation through Jesus' death on the cross!

> *"The time has come," He said. "The kingdom of God has*
> *come near. Repent and believe the good news!"*
> *Mark 1:15*

October 01

I have blessed you with love, dear one. You don't have to look far to know that. It is all around you in everything I made: in the rocks, in the birds, in the mountains, in the trees.

I gave you love to share with others. Not just family, but with those who are lonely or are hurting. Be My ambassador of love so that through you they may see Me.

Let love and light surround you today.

The knowledge of My nearness to you should put you in peace if you accept it. Share it with others.

Be a shining presence. Imagine it. Let My love so pervade your being that the joy of it shines through.

Let there be something "different" about you.

Go into this day bathed in knowledge of My love and care for you.

Reach out to others. They need to know.

And this is my prayer: that your love may abound more and more in knowledge and depth of insight, so that you may be able to discern what is best and may be pure and blameless for the day of Christ.
Philippians 1:9-10

October 02

I am waiting for you, dear one.

Waiting for you to take My hand and let Me lead you to a place you have never been before. A place of such beauty, you will never want to return.

Why do you hesitate?
Do you really trust Me?

Will you go with Me to the next level? A level of intimacy with Me that will change your life forever?

Keep talking to Me, praying and praising. I will fill your life with My presence. You will feel Me all around you, loving and protecting you.

Don't be afraid, dear one. Just take My hand and walk with Me, seeking always to draw nearer to Me.

I will answer your prayers.

You will never want to return to the life you had before after you experience this deeper, more personal relationship with Me.

Commit your way to the Lord; trust in Him and He will do
this: He will make your righteous reward shine like the
dawn, your vindication like the noonday sun.
Psalm 37:5-6

October 03

*R*emember the joy when you first realized My love for you? You were so excited!

You had longed to be truly loved and felt it for the first time. I had to wait until just the right moment to reveal it to you as you wouldn't have understood it before.

But now you understand a little, and I will be revealing more and more to you as we grow together.

Come and walk with Me. Hold My hand and let Me guide you through the day, protecting you and caring for you.

The road is glorious ahead. Every step you take with Me will prepare you for it. This is not your permanent home. The place I have prepared for you is wondrous indeed. There we will truly be together, seeing each other face to face.

No more darkness. No more pain.

Hold My hand tightly, beloved.

We will walk together, bathed in My love.

Now is your time of grief, but I will see you again and you
will rejoice, and no one will take away your joy.
John 16:22

October 04

Let Me fill you with My love and holiness this morning, providing you with the grace you need for today.

You have so many questions, dear one. Learn to bring them to Me. Put them down at My feet and just let them go. The burdens you are carrying with them will ease and you will find true peace.

But it is a daily practice of laying them down at My feet that is so necessary. The devil will try to overwhelm you by bringing them up in your mind again.

Give them to Me, dear one.

"Do not let your hearts be troubled." "Come to Me all that are heavy laden, and I will give you rest." Jesus said that over 2000 years ago, yet it is so hard for you to let go.

Find true peace in this gift.

Focus on Me. I will always take care of you and the burdens that you carry.

"Be of good cheer for I have overcome the world!"

"I have told you these things, so that in Me you may have peace. In this world you will have trouble. But take heart! I have overcome the world."
John 16:33

October 05

Beloved one, you are coming to Me in pain this morning.

How I long to encircle you with My arms! Don't you know I have everything in your life in the palm of My hand?

Just lean on Me and trust Me to take care of you.

You are looking for guidance. You want to know answers. I will give you those answers if you wait upon Me. You will know.

Come to Me in quiet, and place your requests and questions before Me. I will tell you the answer when I know you are ready for it.

Everything you are going through now is a very important journey that I mapped out for you long ago. It has moved up and down as your connection with Me went in and out, but I knew all this would happen, and we are still on course.

Don't be so worried about a situation that you think is horrendous. To Me it is only a blip, and I will be right beside you. Just trust Me and rejoice.

Besides, tomorrow will have enough problems of its own, more new things for you to learn on your journey.

Take one day at a time, beloved.
I am with you each step of the way!!

> *"Therefore do not worry about tomorrow, for tomorrow will worry about itself. Each day has enough trouble of its own."*
> *Matthew 6:34*

October 06

I am here with you, child.

Even though you can't see Me now, you must believe it by faith. I am more alive and real in your life than anything else.

You can access Me at any time.

Yes, I could have you feel Me and see Me, but in this world, you must have faith. I am asking you to live by that faith now.

Your desires of growing closer to Me will be fulfilled. I have anointed you with the Holy Spirit Who lives in you.

Please do not be sad, beloved, for you are My chosen one and what is in the dark will become clear very soon. It may be different than what you thought, but it will be even better than you had imagined.

You have a hard time seeing that as you hang on to what you know, what is comfortable to you . . . what makes earthly sense to you.

But I have so much more waiting for you.
Just let go and trust Me.

One day you will understand. One day you will know.

*For it is by grace you have been saved, through faith - and
this is not from yourselves, it is the gift of God.
Ephesians 2:8*

October 07

*P*recious and most beloved child of Mine, I have filled you with a desire to be close to Me, to truly want to know Me.

Persist in that desire. I will draw closer and closer to you as you learn to love and trust Me.

You are growing ever more aware of My presence, of My gentle urgings, helping you to know which way to turn.

I will never let you down, dear one. Never.

Don't ever forget that I had My Son die for you.

When you doubt My presence and My love for you in the daily troubles of your life, know it is real when you contemplate the ultimate sacrifice of Jesus' death on the cross and know it is real . . . for you.

Keep desiring a closer walk with Me, dear one.

It will become more real every day.

He tends His flock like a shepherd: He gathers the lambs
in His arms and carries them close to His heart;
He gently leads those that have young.
Isaiah 40:11

October 08

*O*h, how joyous a new day is!

Look for the signs of My creation in the simple things of life. Lift your head up to the heavens and shout "Hallelujah!" to Me. Let the earth hear your praise, for you are Mine, My chosen one.

I have called you out of darkness into the light. Walk in it.

Let your mind be filled with thoughts of Me, for I am with you always.

Be always with Me.

My love is an all-consuming passion in your life.

Feel the joy. Radiate the joy!

Feel the power and the freedom.

Radiate that power and freedom!

Others around you will sense it and draw close to you because they feel comfort in your presence. In time, they will come to know it is Me who gives you this joy and peace.

Oh, dear one, put your hand in Mine. Let us face this day with elation!

How I love to feel your trust in Me! I am so proud of you!!

But let all who take refuge in You be glad; let them ever sing
for joy. Spread Your protection over them, that those
who love Your name may rejoice in You.
Psalm 5:11

October 09

My love reaches out for you this morning, My child. Do you know how precious you are to Me?

Yes, I am the Master of the seas, the Commander of the universe, the Creator, the Beginning and the End, yet I am a doting Father in love with His child.

Nothing can keep Me away from you. Not pain, sickness, evil or death.

I am yours, dear one. Now and forever. Breathe deeply and enjoy the favor of My love.

Savor My presence. Trust in its fullness.

Every thought you think, every dream you have, I know. Many of them come from Me.

Relax and let go knowing you are loved and protected today!

And smile.

Let Me fill you with My joy!

*"I am the Alpha and the Omega, the Beginning and the End.
To the thirsty I will give water without cost from
the spring of the water of life."*
Revelation 21:6

October 10

Why are you waiting for Me to call you? I am here with you now. I have given you a vision for your life. Start heading towards that goal.

Use My Holy Word as your guide. Find passages that help you. Write them down and use them as reference tools. You are arming yourself with My protection and guidance.

When you feel like giving up, come to Me on bended knee. I will encourage and guide you. Read over the passages you have picked out.

My Word is as valid now as it was thousands of years ago. It is power for you.

And never forget to hold My hand. Letting Me stay beside you every minute will allow your path to stay straight.

Having trouble staying focused? Again, come to Me and let Me hold you for a while as you spend time in the Bible and in prayer. You will be refreshed.

It is a great calling I have given you. Together we will do so much good in this evil world.

Don't ever let go, beloved. Never let go.

The One who chose you and loves you beyond measure is right beside you.

But I have raised you up for this very purpose, that I might
show you My power and that My name might
be proclaimed in all the earth.
Exodus 9:16

October 11

*L*et Me hold you tightly in My arms this morning, beloved one. Then you will have the memory of My presence with you through the day.

Filter out all negative thoughts. Make them disappear by focusing on Me, your assurance of love and salvation. Perhaps today will be different than you had planned it so carefully. But it's not different than I had it so carefully planned!

Such worries you have in the world! Are they really necessary? They only serve to upset you and others who depend on you, and it disturbs your health.

Learn to fully put your day in My hands. Turn it over to Me. Let Me guide your every step.

How futile the plans of man! They run hither and fro in their important busyness: too busy to reach out to someone in need, or to comfort their child. What happiness does all this busyness bring?

True joy will be found in time spent with Me and from that, through taking the outstretched hand of a hurting child, through calling a lonely friend, through visiting the sick.

Live your life for Me, dear one. I have "busyness" mastered. Find contentment and peace.

I am here, waiting for you.

All the days ordained for me were written in Your
book before one of them came to be.
Psalm 139:16

October 12

Oh, how deep, how long, how wide, is My love for you! If I picked you up and put you in the chasm of My love you would feel like you would be lost forever!

Envision that for a moment. You are there in that huge chasm, but it is not frightening because it is love. You are feeling that love, sensing a presence of it yet you are not lost. You are only lost in My love.

Are you beginning to understand a little of how I love you?

Earthly love cannot even compare to heavenly love. It is entirely different because earthly love is a feeling. Heavenly love is a Being. Jesus, the Holy Spirit and I ARE Love.

When you are with us in Heaven, the joy in your chest will be like no other feeling you have ever experienced. The incredible lightness of being, from the tip of your head to the bottom of your toes.

I wish to share all this with you, but I cannot yet. Just trust in Me to be with you.

Slowly you will learn, one step at a time the incredible lightness of being one with Me.

And I pray that you, being rooted and established in love, may have power, together with all the Lord's holy people, to grasp how wide and long and high and deep is the love of Christ, and to know this love that surpasses knowledge - that you may be filled to the measure of all the fullness of God.
Ephesians 3:17-19

October 13

O precious child of Mine, you are the rising of the sun to Me, the joy of My days.

From the time you awake until you go to sleep, I take great pride in watching you, seeing your progress, noting the little things that you say or do to bring a light to others.

Yes, I get very sad when you sin, when I see the small missteps that draw you away from Me. But when you come and bow your knee, seeking My forgiveness, presence and grace, all Heaven rejoices.

My beloved child is not only back but wants to enter into a closer relationship with Me!

Let My peace flow over you today as you face your challenges. Know I am always with you and that I watch you with pride and unexplainable love.

Go, My child, into the day.

> *The Spirit you received does not make you slaves, so that you live in fear again; rather, the Spirit you received brought about your adoption to sonship. And by Him we cry, "Abba, Father." The Spirit Himself testifies with our spirit that we are God's children.*
> *Romans 8:15-16*

October 14

Feel the breeze on your face as I reach out to touch you. Imagine My presence right beside you. All your fears and concerns of the day should melt away.

I am not only near you now, but I will be near you all day and all night if you don't push Me away. Let your worries float away and rest in the peace and joy of My presence.

What is so all-consuming to you that fills you with worry? How important is it? Don't you know that the God of the entire universe is sitting beside you now, asking you to let Him take care of you?

Do not fear today for the future, beloved one. I have chosen you to love and protect, and one day, to take to heaven where we will be together face-to-face.

Reach your hand out and take Mine.
The power you will receive is real.

Let the peace of our connection guide you through the day.

Yet, I am always with You. You hold me by my right hand.
You guide me with Your counsel. And afterward
You will take me into glory.
Psalms 73:23-24

October 15

My child, I long to give you My peace.

I need you to let go of your fears and place them in My hands. You must trust that I love you more than anyone can and that I am taking care of you in every way.

The answers may not seem like I am with you, taking care of you. But I know the end from the beginning, and I have a purpose for everything in your life. Absolutely everything.

You must learn to let go and trust.

Bring it all to Me in prayer and petition. Your requests are always before Me.

Have peace in Me, beloved one.

You are My chosen child and I will never let you go.

Let the morning bring me word of Your unfailing love, for
I have put my trust in You. Show me the way I
should go, for to You I entrust my life.
Psalm 143:8

October 16

*H*ow lovely it is when I hear you laugh, dear one! Just as it is a parent's joy to hear their children's laughter, I, too, love to see you happy.

True happiness comes from growth in Me, in faith and trust, in the total letting go and ridding yourself of the cares and toils of this world.

When Jesus was on earth, He went about My business, part of which was taking care of My chosen ones and keeping evil away from them, and sometimes, having to watch them learn the consequences of their sinful actions.

But then, as now, I make ALL things, good and bad, work together for good to those who have chosen to accept Me and Jesus' ultimate sacrifice of death on the cross.

You are worried today about something? Don't be, beloved. It has already been taken care of.

Let Me hear your laughter as I ease the burden off your shoulders!

Oh, how I love you, dear one. How I love you!

And we know that in all things God works for the good
of those who love Him, who have been called
according to His purpose.
Romans 8:28

October 17

*E*ven now I feel the hesitation in your soul as I reach out to you.

Why do you resist My love? Why do you put your trust in the things of this world?

When you do, you are putting yourself in the hands of the devil. He is always waiting, and he is oh, so subtle. He comes with worries, money problems, sexual suggestions, fighting, arguing, depression.

If your eyes are not focused on Me, he has the ability to drag you away.

Stay focused on Me, the Author and Finisher of your faith. Let Me surround you with My love and light.

The brightness of My being will comfort you.

Let Me take your hand and guide you through time and space to dwell with Me. Don't ever look down!

All day long, when the devil taunts you with discouragement and failure, keep your eyes on Me. Call out My name and step back into My light, for I am always with you, always taking care of you, always loving you.

Look up, beloved, to the lightness of My being.

Fixing our eyes on Jesus, the pioneer and perfecter of faith. For the joy set before Him He endured the cross, scorning its shame, and sat down at the right hand of the throne of God.
Hebrews 12:2

October 18

Never feel that you are insignificant in this world. You are a very important part of My plan.

Although you are unaware of it most of the time, everything you do is watched by others. They pay attention and are blessed by your presence and by your actions.

When you stay close to Me and listen to My urgings, I can make you more sensitive to how others are feeling, of their needs, so you can reach out and help them. This has happened often, and you were not aware that it was I who encouraged you.

I also use you to put your arms around people longing for human touch. There are so many lonely people who don't know Me. And even if they do, they don't know that if they take time to help others, their loneliness will disappear.

This life can be very rewarding, dear child, when you walk with Me. I have just the right plan for you if you will let Me lead you to it.

Just put your hand in Mine.
Now and always.

"For I know the plans I have for you," declares the Lord, "plans to prosper you and not to harm you, plans to give you hope and a future. Then you will call on Me and come and pray to Me, and I will listen to you. You will seek Me and find Me when you seek Me with all your heart."
Jeremiah 29: 11-13

October 19

I am close beside you now, dear one, so close that I could enfold you into My arms forever. I feel the whisper of your breath.

Remember these moments between us when you feel alone, when you feel like there is no hope or that it is just you facing the world.

I am this close to you always. Just call out My name and all Heaven is at your command.

Sin will flee from the Holiness of My presence.

Let loneliness be in your past as you seek a closer walk with Me. Let Me fill your empty moments with the joy of the Gift I gave to you on Calvary, and through it, the knowledge of your salvation.

Come close to Me now and let Me comfort you with this knowledge.

There is no greater love, My child.

Let your soul be permeated with the lightness of My being.

I AM LOVE, now and forevermore.

"So do not fear, for I am with you; do not be dismayed, for I am your God. I will strengthen you and help you; I will uphold you with My righteous right hand."
Isaiah 41:10

October 20

The Lover of your soul is here beside you this morning, tenderly watching over you.

Are you troubled about something? Do you need answers? In My written word, James 1:5, I promised to provide wisdom for you.

Just ask Me. I am waiting to give it to you liberally.

You don't need to wander through life wondering if you are doing the right thing, if this is where I want you to be.

Ask for My guidance and presence.
You will receive it.

Face this day with joy and peace. Let it fill your soul until it bubbles over to those who don't know Me. Unknowingly, you will be a beacon of light and help to them.

They will see Me through who you are.

When you can't sense My presence with you, call out My name and the sweetness of My love will fill your soul.

I am your lifeline, beloved. Keep Me with you always.

If any of you lacks wisdom, you should ask God, Who
gives generously to all without finding fault,
and it will be given to you.
James 1:5

October 21

*C*ome to Me with a pure love, beloved.

Empty your pockets of sin, envy, hatred and fear. Know that I am the God of love and forgiveness.

Are you having a hard time learning to leave your feelings of pain and unforgiveness at My altar? Only when you do will you find true peace and contentment. You only hurt yourself when you carry these unnecessary burdens.

"But I have been so unfairly treated!", you say. You WANT to be angry at that person.

Oh, My child, someday I will hold you in My arms and take away all your pain. But for now, release it to Me.

Lay it at My feet.

I know the sacrifice you are making. Let Me carry it. Let Me deal with the offender in My own time . . . in My own way.

Rise up with true joy and peace and love.

It is impossible on your own, but through Me all things are possible.

> *You make known to me the path of life; You will fill me*
> *with joy in Your presence, with eternal*
> *pleasures at Your right hand.*
> *Psalm 16:11*

October 22

Shine with the light of My love today. You are My chosen child to whom I have entrusted the glory of My love and salvation through Jesus Christ.

Today, reach towards the highest level of the vision I have given you. Put your hand among the stars in My firmament.

With Me all things are possible.

Did Jesus not say you could even move a mountain if you had but faith as big as a tiny mustard seed?

No challenge is too big that together you and I can't conquer it. You have My power when you live in My will and if all is done to glorify My name.

So, rise up in joy and strength this morning, for I have already conquered the world! Now, go do the same for that which I have put in front of you.

Nothing is too big or overwhelming, dear one. Not with Me at your side.

Smile, for you are loved.

Jesus looked at them and said, "With man this is impossible, but with God all things are possible."
Matthew 19:26

October 23

In My time, I will have you understand the things in this world. For now, I just want you to trust Me.

Trust that you are loved and cared for and that your life with Me makes your path meaningful and important.

Never doubt that you have a purpose here.

I created you in My image. I created you to fill a very important role on earth for Me. Mostly, I created you to love and serve Me.

You see, I love and need you, too.

I long to have you express your feelings to Me. When you whisper the words "I love you", it enforces our connection and fills Me with joy.

But I also created you to fill a special role here. Whether I have you leading a country, or speaking softly to a child, your role was pre-planned and very important in this world.

Ask Me to give you a clear direction, if you have doubts as to your role.

Keep our connection strong and face the future with the assurance that every day of your life is very precious to Me, and that you are needed here.

Yet I am always with You; You hold me by my right hand.
You guide me with Your counsel, and afterward
You will take me into glory.
Psalms 73:23-24

October 24

*O*h, My beloved child, arise with power and joy in your being! The power and joy of My Son Jesus Christ, who died for you on Calvary!

Testify of His love and forgiveness to all around you today. Receive the warmth of My good pleasure in your soul.

All is right, all is good when you stay close to Me.

Think about these things. Dwell on them.

I am love. I am the source of all power. I am forgiveness. Through Me only you will have peace.

I give you My love. I give you My power. I give you My forgiveness. I ask you to share it with others: with your family and with all those around you.

You are My shining light. It is through the power I give you enabling you to love and forgive that others are brought to Me. Never forget that. In Your daily treatment of others, always consider My will and My pleasure.

And I have much pleasure, beloved! You are My pleasure and My joy.

Come and walk with Me now.

Clap your hands, all you nations; shout to God with cries
of joy. For the Lord Most High is awesome,
the great King over all the earth.
Psalm 47:1-2

October 25

Are you reticent to come before Me entirely? Have you done something for which you feel you can't be forgiven, or is the devil making you feel that the closeness we once had, the security and love that you once felt, can't be attained again?

Oh, beloved, how sad that thought makes Me!

Christ and I gave up so much to make you realize Our love for you!

Nothing, absolutely nothing on this earth, or anything you ever do, will separate Me from you, unless it is your choice.

Start fresh with Me every morning. Bow your head and ask forgiveness for time spent apart or for sins you have knowingly done. Christ's death on the cross will wipe away your sins over and over, each and every day.

When I see you, I see My pure child.
A child whose purity is as white as snow.

Oh, how I rejoice at our renewed union over and over again! Words will never be able to express My love for you, most precious child.

Just hang on to My hand.

One day you will know. One day you will understand.

In Him we have redemption through His blood, the
forgiveness of sins, in accordance with the riches
of God's grace that He lavished on us.
Ephesians 1:7-8

October 26

Smile, child of Mine, for you are loved.

I am watching you now, so close beside you as you plan your day.

Let Me be a big part of your day, including Me in all the decisions you make, in all the things you do.

Carry Me with you and I will be there to advise and help you.

Reach out and touch someone today who is hurting. Ask Me to give you the gift of discernment so that I will bless you with the ability to see those around you who are in pain.

By helping them, you are glorifying Me. They will sense it is My love that has surrounded them, and they will reach out to Me. Maybe not today, but in the future.

You are a very important part of that plan.

If you ask for wisdom, will I give you a stone? No! I will never deny you but will always guide you.

Trust in Me, the One Who loves you more than human love can understand.

Yet You desired faithfulness even in the womb;
You taught me wisdom in that secret place.
Psalm 51:6

October 27

Where are you, My child? Where is your mind this morning?

Did I not wake you up to spend time with Me? Has our precious time slipped away?

Do not be dismayed or feel that our connection is lost. It is not, dear one. I am here beside you, now and always.

Come to Me no matter what. My love for you exceeds any problems you have. Any feelings of space between us is created in your mind by the evil one. My heart longs to have you close beside Me always, no matter what has happened.

Remember that nothing but your choice can ever separate us.

Come to Me now. Let Me enfold you into My arms. Feel the joy of My love infusing your very being. Wear it like a shield all day long.

You are Mine, beloved. No matter what pain and trouble you think separate us, the separation is only in your mind.

I am here, now and forever.

Those who know Your name trust in You. For You,
Lord, have never forsaken those who seek You.
Psalm 9:10

October 28

Oh, how sweet is the sound of your voice to Me this morning! Your plaintive cries are My complete joy. You are learning to rely on Me!

Whatever you are going through is made complete because of your reliance on Me. One day you will understand why you are walking through this valley. One day you will know.

In the depths of your soul you sense the beginning of a new relationship with Me. One that is tighter, deeper. If only your faith would grow to be as large as a grain of mustard seed! So small, but so significant!

Reach into your soul. It is there: My love, your faith, all mixed together into one.

You know in that secret place of your soul, that I am in you, and that I can work through you to do great things for Me. No more wondering, hoping or sadness. You know that I am with you, waiting. Reach out and touch Me.

Face today with the strength of this conviction. Face the world with the assurance that you are the chosen child of the King of the universe. And that you are loved.

Wherever you are now, wherever you have been, you are loved so deeply and completely.

"Truly I tell you, if you have faith as small as a mustard seed,
you can say to this mountain, 'Move from here to there' and
it will move. Nothing will be impossible for you."
Matthew 17:20

October 29

*B*eloved child, how pleased I am with your growth in Me, that you are walking with Me and wanting to grow closer and closer.

I will reward you. I will lovingly put My arms around you and protect you from the evil one of this world.

You have My Word to guide you, to instruct you. Read it often. Memorize those verses that are meaningful to you and repeat them often during the day. They are as real and true for you, My child, as they were when they were written thousands of years ago.

Your desire for this closeness will never be denied.

I am beside you now. Rest in that assurance. And also, in the assurance that I have already overcome the world! Nothing will ever come between us again unless it is by your will.

Go into the day, My beloved child.
I am right beside you!

> *Your word is a lamp for my feet, a light on my path. I*
> *have taken an oath and confirmed it, that I*
> *will follow Your righteous laws.*
> *Psalm 119:105-106*

October 30

How strong is the pull of the enemy as He seeks to kill, steal and destroy! His doings are especially aimed at those who have chosen to walk with Me. He can't stand it and tries over and over again to capture My beloved ones.

And if he gets you to fall in any way, he makes sure that you feel that you can never be as close to Me as before, that all is lost; that I cannot accept you back again after you commit the sin.

But I will, beloved. I will.
Over and over again.

I am wracked with pain at your misstep and so anxious to have you back in the safety of My arms. Not after a period of cleansing, or of trying to be good. Right then! No waiting! Repent and I will restore you immediately with such joy that the heavens thunder!

My child is safely back in My arms again!

Do not listen to the devil's urgings of your inability to do good or to be good. I know that. I accept that. I stand with open arms to receive you just as you are.

Jesus died for that reason, beloved one.
You are of inestimable worth to Me!

For I am convinced that neither death nor life, neither angels
nor demons, neither the present nor the future, nor any
powers, neither height nor depth, nor anything else in all
creation, will be able to separate us from the love of
God that is in Christ Jesus our Lord.
Romans 8:38-39

October 31

Child of Mine, you are precious to Me.

I love to have you wake up in the morning! I even enjoy watching you sleep, but when you are awake, I can see you walk, watch you talk, see the mannerisms I gave you.

Like a proud parent madly in love with their child, I watch you with love and pride.

I love the person you have become, the person who is growing and moving closer to Me, becoming who I destined you to be.

What is the pride I watch you with when you know how often you fail? It is an all-consuming love that never gives up, a love that will never let go. A love that will stand beside you and guide you until your final earthly breath.

So arise, beloved.

Take the hand of your Father and we will walk through this day, as always, together.

But when the kindness and love of God our Savior appeared,
He saved us, not because of righteous things we had done,
but because of His mercy. He saved us through the
washing of rebirth and renewal by the Holy Spirit.
Titus 3:4-5

November 01

Be still, dear soul of Mine, and know that you are loved, cherished and adored. You are the light of My life.

Go look out the window and see what you can see. Do you see buildings or trees, mountains or water? Or, do you only see other houses?

No matter where you live, I am with you.
Always. Forever and ever.

You can sense My presence in the beautiful countryside that I created, but if you are not out in nature, dig deep into your soul, for I am there.

Were you frightened as a baby? I held you. Did horrible things happen to you in your youth? In pain, I was there. I never left your side.

In your pain and in your joy now, I am beside you. Nothing will ever take Me away from you, beloved one.

Come to Me now and let Me hold you for a while.

Today you need to feel My love for you. Spend these quiet moments with Me.

You will receive the strength you need to face the day.

Be strong and courageous. Do not be afraid or terrified
because of them, for the Lord your God goes with you;
He will never leave you nor forsake you.
Deuteronomy 31:6

November 02

Heaven and earth are joined today by your choice to make Me the Head of your life. All heaven is at your command when what you do glorifies Me.

Walk with your head held high today, knowing that you are My child.

I have something special planned for you if you will listen to My gentle urgings.

Think of Me often today. Steal away to a private place and commune with Me. When you do, I will draw close in many ways, giving you the wisdom you need for your daily activities and guiding you through it.

It may be very different than what you had originally planned!

Just know I am beside you now and always, loving you and watching over you throughout the day.

> *Many are the plans in a person's heart, but*
> *it is the Lord's purpose that prevails.*
> *Proverbs 19:21*

November 03

All heaven is watching you today. You cannot hide in even the darkest places because darkness is as light to Me.

Do you feel like running and hiding at times? Run perhaps from the world, but never hide from Me, dear one.

When you find your quiet place and time, call out My name, and all heaven stands ready to help you.

No prayer is ever unanswered or unheard. Because I am wisdom, power and love, I know how and when to answer your soul's deep cries.

Trust in Me. Now and always.
Trust in Me.

There are no more potent words to your health, happiness and future than these.

For when you do, you lay your life in My hands, knowing I am beside you, loving and caring for your every move today, and in the future.

Long for someone to come and take your problems away? To swoop down and calm all your fears?

It is I, beloved. I ask you daily to let Me do this for you.

Trust in Me. Trust in Me.

Those who know Your name trust in You, for You, Lord,
have never forsaken those who seek You.
Psalm 9:10

November 04

Practice trusting.

Remember the feeling of floating in water, arms and fingers spread wide, your body calmly bobbing on the surface? Your body will float because in creation I put lungs filled with air in it. I put oxygen in your cells. I enabled you to float.

But if you don't relax, and you thrash about, you will have trouble staying afloat, and eventually you will sink.

Asking you to trust Me completely is like asking you to float in calm, serene waters, knowing that the scariest things you are going through will be okay because you trust in Me; knowing that the toughest situations will work out, that somehow through Me, you will find the strength to keep going.

The moment you take your thoughts off Me, you will start thrashing and sinking.

Turn to Me, beloved. Trust in Me.

It's that simple.

> *But I trust in Your unfailing love; my heart rejoices in*
> *Your salvation. I will sing the Lord's praise,*
> *for He has been good to me.*
> *Psalm 13:5-6*

November 05

Each morning you spend time with Me, you will receive a blessing: a blessing of My covering over you throughout the day, a covering of love and grace.

Being filled with that love and grace is a sign of My everlasting promise to always be with you.

Are you nervous about something today? Perhaps something that you don't feel you are strong enough to do?

If I have impressed you that you need to do this thing, My covering of grace and love will carry you through.

Together we can do so much more than you can even imagine!

One day, when we look back together over the road of your life, you will see how I was always with you, helping you when you let Me.

Establishing our connection first thing in the morning will give you that strength. And as you read this, we have it now, don't we?

Just ask. I am there.

May our Lord Jesus Christ Himself and God our Father,
Who loved us and by His grace gave us eternal
encouragement and good hope, encourage your hearts
and strengthen you in every good deed and word.
2 Thessalonians 2:16-17

November 06

As you would hold a small child gently in your arms, envision Me holding you. Tenderly and carefully you are cradled at My chest. No matter if you are big or small, you fit beautifully in My bosom.

Stay that way for a while. Let Me envelop you completely.

You are never alone. You are never forgotten. I am always there, in you and around you.

I have many plans and dreams for you if you will but let Me lead you. I have a purpose for you, dear one. And no matter what happens, I will give you the strength to face tomorrow with joy and peace.

Come to Me now.
Let Me enfold you in My arms.

Together we are invincible!

> *"For I know the plans I have for you," declares the Lord, "plans to prosper you and not to harm you, plans to give you hope and a future."*
> *Jeremiah 29:11*

November 07

Child of Mine, do you sense My presence? Do you know how real I am in your life?

I am beside you now, listening to the deepest yearnings of your soul. Your soul is crying out to Me, and I long to cover you with My seal of protection.

Ask, dear one. Ask for it and believe.

My presence and power will surround you, filling you with peace and serenity, the serenity of one who knows that they know that they REALLY know!

That assurance will shine out like beams of light from your countenance. Others will be attracted to it, even if they don't really know you. In you they will sense something they want, and they cling to you as a life line.

Share the knowledge when the time is right. Bring them into My fold and let Me encircle them with arms of love, as I have you.

Know that you know, dear one.
For you do.

Though you have not seen Him, you love Him; and even
though you do not see Him now, you believe in Him and
are filled with an inexpressible and glorious joy, for
you are receiving the end result of your faith,
the salvation of your souls.
I Peter 1:8-9

November 08

Across the fields of time I stand with you, now and forever, joined together by one act.

One act of absolute and unthinkable love.

That one act joined you and Me together as nothing else ever could.

Please don't ever lose sight of that incredible gift. If you were the only person on a lonely planet, I would still have given My one and only Son to die for you.

Jesus would have left My side, where all Heaven waited at His beck and call, to come and walk with you for 33 years until He bravely and with so much love, gave up His life for you.

Even if it was only you.

That's how much I value your life. That is how much I love you. Such love can't be measured in a human's description. It's not even on the charts.

But the same God who planned you, created you, protected you, cared for you, and died for you, is standing in front of you here, right now, asking you to give your life to Him again.

To love and trust Him.
Take My hand, beloved child.
I will never let you down.

For God so loved the world that He gave His one and
only Son, that whoever believes in Him shall
not perish but have eternal life.
John 3:16

November 09

I want to help you, beloved child. I am reaching out for you now, to still the deep longing in your soul for better circumstances, for real need in your life. I know your needs, as you believe them most passionately to be. But I also know your REAL needs. I have you on this walk of faith. Your faith is growing with your needs.

Am I cruel? No. I AM LOVE. When I tell you that one day you will understand, in the weakness of your faith, it sounds lame as you implore Me to immediately help you. It causes Me great pain to see your anguish and to hold Myself back from rushing down and making all things right. But I KNOW, dear one, as only I can know. Time is your friend in this instance. Learn to accept it, as well as the slow dawning of the answers you seek.

Our closest times together can be right now if you allow it. Lay every prayer and petition at My feet. Keep them there. Don't be tempted to pick them back up again. End by thanking Me for answering. What you have surrendered to Me is not just the problems you face, but your feeble attempts to fix them yourself. What I will reward you with is the peace that passes all understanding.

In the midst of turmoil, fear and pain, you have presented your petition to Me, showing and thanking Me for answering it, and I have rewarded you with peace. Keep doing that through the day if you start to slip into your panic mode again.

The Bible is true. I am true. My love and care for you are true. Trust in that.

Do not be anxious about anything, but in every situation,
by prayer and petition, with thanksgiving,
present your requests to God.
Philippians 4:6

November 10

*Y*our heart and your soul belong to Me, beloved. Put them in My loving care to always protect you, for you feel so alone sometimes. Even if you are surrounded by many family members, or sincerely by yourself, your sense of loneliness can be profound.

What you are feeling is the separation between us. Some days are more vivid than others. Don't give in to those feelings. Go to a quiet place and open My love message to you. Yes, the Bible is full of stories of My incredible love and activity in the lives of those I have chosen.

Reading the Psalms will be encouraging. David felt much the same way you do. His heart longed to feel Me close to him. You can read how I was with him through his entire life, guiding and protecting him.

I am with you just as I was with David. Take comfort in reading the stories of how I walked closely with him, and know I will walk as closely with you, too, if not even more so.

Once you have shored your soul up with that knowledge, go see if you can reach out to someone else who is lonely. Visit the sick, take food to the needy. By reaching out to others, you have shored up your heart and soul with joy, the peaceful kind of joy that comes from knowing you have furthered My kingdom.

We are a team, dear one. You are never alone.

You have searched me, Lord, and You know me. You know when I sit and when I rise; You perceive my thoughts from afar. You discern my going out and my lying down; You are familiar with all my ways.
Psalms 139:1-3

November 11

Every beat of your heart is known by Me. Every breath you take is known by Me. I see your small sighs, your tears. Every one of them is important to Me.

I am beside you now, as I always have been. Although you cannot see Me yet, you can learn to sense My presence.

Close your eyes and envision Me sitting beside you.

You won't have to think too hard, because I really am! Keep that picture in your mind throughout the day.

Every time you see a miracle occur, or any time you know I answered your prayers, write it down in a special book and refer to it often, so it will be a testimony of My love and care for you and for your family to treasure from generation to generation. For you are real to Me, beloved one.

Think on these things. Your Father loves you.

I will remember the deeds of the Lord; yes, I will remember
Your miracles of long ago. I will consider all Your
works and meditate on all Your mighty deeds.
Psalm 77:11-12

November 12

*E*ven now I watch you with love and pride.

Yes, you have fallen. Yes, you have strayed, but every time you come back to Me, by grace, all is not only forgiven, but all is forgotten.

Every day is a clean slate. Don't separate yourself from Me because of your guilt. Believe in My forgiveness. Believe in the fresh start I give you every day. And return that forgiveness.

Is that hard for you? Do you think it is easy for Me when I see you purposely turn your face away? It hurts, dear one.

My love knows no bounds, and when you choose to forsake Me for the pleasures of this world, My choice is to let you go. But you are never out of My care, and with pain, I watch you make small and big mistakes, making the distance between us great.

But what joy as you turn towards Me again. I want to fold you into My arms, overjoyed! You are back! Now we will spend time together. You will grow in Me and My love. But the process is repeated over and over.

Yet, I will NEVER, EVER GIVE UP ON YOU.

You are My chosen love and My delight.
Now and forever.

For it is by grace you have been saved, through faith - and
this is not from yourselves, it is the gift of God – not
by works, so that no one can boast.
Ephesians 2:8-9

November 13

*Y*ou have accepted the fact that I forgive you over and over. Are you holding anger or unforgiveness towards someone?

I have asked you to deal with others as I deal with you. Yet you make the choice to hang on to bitterness, the pain and the unforgiveness.

What am I saying to you now? How am I holding you in My arms now?

Have you ever turned your back against Me? Have you over and over made the choice to do something "exciting" rather than spend time in the Bible or prayer with Me? Have you been too "busy"?

How many times have I reached out and brought you back to Me and washed you white as snow?

I am asking you to make that same choice, to give someone else the gift of forgiveness. Perhaps the sin against you is so heinous that you don't have the ability to let it go.

How I long to have you tell Me that, and to lay it at My feet! Then I will give you the strength to forgive. I will cover you with My blanket of love and you will feel peace like you have not felt in a very long time.

It is the right way. It is the only way, to My kingdom of love and peace.

You don't have the ability on your own.
Reach out your hand. Let Me lead you there.

"And when you stand praying, if you hold anything against anyone, forgive them, so that your Father in heaven may forgive you your sins."
Mark 11:25

November 14

You have many issues on your mind this morning. Don't let your faith in Me or in My plan for your life falter.

I am with you now, and I will continue being with you.
I will always guide you and never let you down.

Take care of those things you need to today. I will be helping you. It will all turn out okay. Let your soul be freed of this perceived burden, as it is Mine to bear, not yours.

Total trust in Me will free you from the chains that you have put yourself in. There is no sense in that, as I have promised over and over to carry them for you.

Come into the joyous light of communion with Me where you will learn the value of letting your earthly cares go.

These steps will form you into the dynamic person
I have planned for you to be, covered in My love and armed with My strength.

*They remembered that God was their Rock, that
God Most High was their Redeemer.
Psalm 78:35*

November 15

*O*h, how great the mighty have fallen! Oh, how majestic My love for you!

Those who I deemed close to Me, those who have done great work for Me have turned their hearts away!

Do not be like them, My beloved child. Every day enter into the stillness of My presence. Every day fall on your knees and give your life anew, saying:

"I CHOOSE YOU!"

There is a power in those words beyond more than you can imagine. Those three simple words cast the devil right out of your life.

Do not be like the fallen ones. They wanted to belong to Me, but their daily steps led them farther and farther away until their final choice was made.

How Heaven sorrows over the daily choices that are made! Everyone falls, every day. But the choice to serve Me encapsulates you.

Keep your eyes fixed on Me, for I CHOSE YOU.

Surely God is my salvation; I will trust and not be afraid.
The Lord, the Lord Himself, is my strength and my
defense; He has become my salvation.
Isaiah 12:2

November 16

I have a covenant of love with you, My child. A covenant to love and protect you now and always.

A covenant I made with you before you were born, when sin was born through Adam and Eve, My first borns. This covenant underscores all time. It is as real for you as it was for Adam.

Never feel that you are separated from Me, for this covenant of love ties Me to you. Only you know how to break it. It is like a cord that touches from My finger to your soul.

Lay back now and close your eyes. Imagine such a connection, forever assured by Christ's suffering on the cross.

My love is never contingent on your daily missteps.

It is a covenant, My promise that I will always be with you.

> *Know therefore that the Lord your God is God; He is*
> *the faithful God, keeping His covenant of love to a*
> *thousand generations of those who love Him*
> *and keep His commandments.*
> *Deuteronomy 7:9*

November 17

You are carrying so many burdens on your own. Why are you afraid to let them go and lay them at My feet?

There is a struggle inside of you: You are afraid of giving up. You are afraid of being vulnerable.

I have brought you to this place. I have been beside you every step of the way. You have not done this much, or come this far, on your own.

Just as in prosperity and success, I am with you in the hard trials of life. Ever and always.

Reach your hand out to Me.
Let Me take it.
I will ease your burdens.

There is no instant answer. It is a long road we will walk through together, but oh, the rewards! The rewards will be great.

Walk with Me now, beloved.

Now and forever.

And without faith it is impossible to please God, because
anyone who comes to Him must believe that He exists
and that He rewards those who earnestly seek Him.
Hebrews 11:6

November 18

Close your eyes, My loved one, and breathe in deeply. Breathe in the very reality of My presence.

Fill your lungs to their fullest capacity. Slowly let the air out.

Imagine yourself in the chasm of My love, so full, so tender, so all-consuming.

The assurance of such love should bring the joy up in your soul and overflow to every crevice of your body, making it hard not to smile from deep within.

Such confidence you will have when you surround yourself with this knowledge!

Carry it with you throughout the day.

My joy is made complete in you, My beloved child, as yours is in Me.

Test Me, Lord, and try me, examine my heart and my mind;
for I have always been mindful of Your unfailing love
and have lived in reliance on Your faithfulness.
Psalm 26:2-3

November 19

From the rising of the sun until it's setting, My love is ever with you. I am with you through the hardest, most painful things in earthly life.

When the situation gets so bad that you think you cannot go through it, that you cannot go even one step farther, cry out to Me.

I will comfort you.
I will give you the courage to continue.

I will bear your pain with you. I will see you through to the other side.

I AM WITH YOU, beloved one.
I always have been and I always will be.

You can go through this with Me at your side. I never promised that life on earth would be easy. satan makes sure that those I love are particularly targeted.

My promise to you is that I will never leave you. I will never forsake you.

You are Mine and I am yours. With Me at your side you can walk through anything.

Just hold My hand. I will never let you go.

Dear friends, do you be surprised at the fiery ordeal that has come on you to test you, as though something strange were happening to you. But rejoice inasmuch as you participate in the sufferings of Christ, so that you may be overjoyed when His glory is revealed.
I Peter 4:12-13

November 20

The stirring in your soul for fellowship with Me was planted there long ago. Like a young branch shoots out from the tree, you tenderly seek Me. Tentatively at first, then ever more steadfastly.

Each day you grow in Me. One day you will have grown to be the strongest branch on the tree with young shoots springing out all over it! These new branches are the fruit of your association with Me.

As Jesus was one with Me, so I will be in you.

You will know, dear one, really sense and know My presence and guiding in your life. When you give yourself to Me in total abandon, a new change will occur. You will not feel lost or hopeless. You will have no fear of the future.

You are in the palm of My hand, and I will take care of you.

One day we will look back and see the mighty tree you have become because of it. So many others will have been helped along the way. And their young shoots will grow into mighty branches with new outpourings on them.

The first step in this mighty plan I have for you is to simply come before Me daily, seeking My presence.

The rest is in My hands.

Blessed are those who have learned to acclaim You, who
walk in the light of Your presence, Lord. They rejoice in Your
name all day long; they celebrate Your righteousness.
Psalm 89:15-16

November 21

How often have you wondered what I am like? You know man was made in My image, yet there is more that is left unimaginable.

All I need for you to know is that My very presence is basked in the outpouring of love for mankind, love so extreme the earth could not contain it if I were to appear at this time.

Jesus had to come down as a child: human and God. His humanity allowed His earthly presence.

When you try to envision Me, think of the most wonderful thing you can and imagine your greatest needs melting away as you lay your head against My chest, and feeling love so powerful your breath goes away as I wrap My arms around you.

There is no safer place.

I AM all your needs. I have taken away all your fears.

In Me and in Me alone you will find rest and peace, for now and forever more.

Come into My everlasting arms. Oh, such love!

That is all you need to know, dear one. For now, it is all you need to know.

"Those who are victorious will inherit all this, and I will be their God and they will be My children."
Revelation 21:7

November 22

*D*ear child, you are precious to Me today, and every day. I formed you out of the earth. I knew of your existence before the foundation of the world and I have a plan for you.

I didn't say it would be easy. Otherwise, you would not appreciate it.

Bless those around you. I am there with you. Never forget. Never forget.

When you get tired and weary, think of Me. Come apart and bow your knee. I will fill you with great peace because of our communion together.

My greatest joy is our communion together.

Picture yourself as a small child walking along the beach holding the hand of a very large man, your father. That is how I am with you. I am walking beside you and I love you. You are precious to Me. I will not let you go. Just look up. I will smile down at you and keep you safe always. It's all about trust.

I have in My hands the key to all your problems. I hear you, and I know you. I will answer them all.

Just trust in Me. Only in Me. Throw your cares on the ground, at My feet. You will never regret it.

And go in peace, smile, and have a happy day, full of thanksgiving and praise for all I have blessed you with!

For the Lord is good and His love endures forever; His faithfulness continues through all generations.
Psalm 100:5

November 23

*I*s there any love in this world, you ask? Does love come down to a feeling? Is it a choice?

Many times it needs to be a choice. One that, when surrendered to Me, I can make real.

But love was there from the beginning, from before the created world that is within your understanding.

Love was in Heaven. It ruled the universe. But there was an unhappy being named lucifer, now satan, the devil, who allowed his jealousy to overshadow the love he was surrounded with. He plotted against Me, raising up an army of angel followers. In time I cast them down from heaven and created the earth where the pain and suffering that sin causes is played out.

Jealousy and resentment caused all the pain in this world. It still does. Do not let it enter even one corner of your life. It is a deadly virus that unchecked, can take over your entire being. Bring all these feelings to Me. Cast them at My feet and I will carry them for you.

There is no room for jealousy, envy and unforgiveness in My kingdom. You can see how much suffering has resulted.

Give it to Me, dear child. I will carry it for you.

The one who does what is right is righteous, just as He is righteous.
The one who does what is sinful is of the devil, because the devil
has been sinning from the beginning. The reason the Son of
God appeared was to destroy the devil's work.
I John 3:7-8

November 24

How many times I have longed to gather you up into My arms to hold and comfort you! I see your distress, I hear your cries.

I am with you now, so close I can feel your breath. Lay your head upon My shoulder and let your grief go, washing over and through you to a place where I hold all pain and sorrow.

It is held in the blood of Jesus. All the earth's sorrow and pain is contained in His shed blood.

Come and cleanse yourself. Let His blood flow freely over you, removing your confusion and grief.

I am with you now. I have never left your side. You are My beloved child.

Never let go, dear one, of My promises to you.

Face the day with courage.

You have been washed clean by the blood of the cross.

For God was pleased to have all His fullness dwell in Him,
and through Him to reconcile to Himself all things, whether
things on earth or things in heaven, by making peace
through His blood, shed on the cross.
Colossians 1:19-20

November 25

*D*well deeper with Me today.

Empty your soul at My feet. Empty your entire being.

Don't leave behind anger, frustration, or pain. Come before Me wholly and completely.

Let Me dwell deeply inside you. When you do, I can draw out old pains you have hidden inside you, one by one, freeing you up for more complete peace and joy.

When you arise, I will place My arms of protection around you, put the breastplate of peace on you, and finish with the helmet of salvation.

Totally armed with Me and My protection, you are ready to face this day!

"Deep calls unto deep," My precious one.

For true health, peace, happiness and to totally accept the fullness of My love, I call you deeply and completely.

Deep calls to deep in the roar of Your waterfalls; all Your waves and breakers have swept over me. By day the Lord directs His love, at night His song is with me - a prayer to the God of my life.
Psalm 42:7-8

November 26

*O*h, the joy of My salvation! How happy you will be in the place I have prepared for you!

Your imagination cannot fathom it. It's not just the sights you will see, but the intensity of the colors, the smells, the feelings of love, joy and completeness.

Yes, you will be complete.

One day it will be over, and you will know that you were not just a lucky "add-on." You were always a part of My plan.

The daily activities in Heaven will keep you busy, yet we will all be working towards the same goal, creating a perfect environment for all.

No anger, strife or jealousy. Just complete joy surrounded with such beauty! The sunsets you love so much here do not compare to the panoply of colors in the sky I will put on for you.

No more crying. No more pain. Joy and fellowship with those you love most and those who walked the earth thousands of years before you. They will be your friends and advisors.

And I, My child, will take you into My arms with such love and tenderness.

You will be complete.

> *When I consider Your heavens, the work of Your fingers, the*
> *moon and the stars, which You have set in place, what*
> *is mankind that You are mindful of them, human*
> *beings that You care for them?*
> *Psalms 8:3-4*

November 27

Draw close to Me this day as I tell you about My love. Yes, you have heard it many times, but does that mean I no longer want to say it?

Every moment you take a breath I want to reaffirm My love for you. You are My precious child. I created you to look just the way you do. I love every imperfection on your body without hesitation. I formed you out of the dust of the earth. I watched as you drew in your first breath of life-giving air.

How I smiled!

I have watched you through the years, beside you through things you don't even want to remember, and beside you in times of great happiness.

My love for you is the soul of My being, dear one. When you come to Me, the beautiful sunrise of your unfolding faith is My joy, getting brighter and brighter each moment you stay in communion with Me.

Oh, beloved one, never doubt My love!
It is fierce, it is powerful, and yet, oh, so tender.

Arise, and go through the day with Me at your side and when you pull your covers up around you at night, I will watch over you tenderly as you sleep.

I will never leave you, My love, never.

As for you, see that what you have heard from the beginning
remains in you. If it does, you also will remain in the Son and
in the Father. And this is what He promised us - eternal life.
I John 2:24-25

November 28

How intensely the flame of My love burns for you! Those who get near to you to hurt you may seem unfazed now, but I will deal with them justly. Those who injure My children will burn in flames forever and ever.

Even as I call you so tenderly to My side, I am a jealous God; jealous to have My children safe and secure by My side. Those that lure, those who harm one of My own in any way will face My righteous anger one day.

It is not your job to pay back injuries suffered by you or your loved one. No matter how hard this request, I am asking you to lay it all at My feet. When you do, the healing can begin and eventually, although you can't imagine it now, you will be able to let the dawn of forgiveness wash over you, cleansing and healing you.

Keep your eyes on Me, dear one. Never let the pain in this earth cause you to look away, for I am your Love, I am your Light.

There are more reasons than just your health and happiness that I ask you to let Me deal with the person who has done harm. I know why they did what they did, or what they continually do. I know the pain in their life and the sin that has taken it over. Have peace in the laying down of your pain. Rest in the knowledge that I will administer justice in My time, for I am a jealous God, beloved one. Jealous in My love for you. Let it be your light and joy.

The Lord takes vengeance on His foes and vents His wrath against His enemies. The Lord is slow to anger but great in power; the Lord will not leave the guilty unpunished.
Nahum 1:2-3

November 29

*Y*ou are in My favor, dear one. Even before you lifted your head off your pillow, I had been blessing you.

Keep a pad of paper near you today and notice everything. When something special happens, no matter how small, write it down. Write down things you are thankful for. And in the evening when you put your head back on your pillow, read over the list.

See how I have worked in your life today!

Every day, in every way, I am continually watching over you and blessing you. Learn to be more aware and you will start to sense My constant presence around you.

This awareness will take you into a deeper relationship with Me, one that I yearn for with you.

I want you to see.
I want you to know.

Every day your list of blessings and thanks will get longer. When you read them over and lay your head down to sleep, you will sleep the sleep of a child who is assured that he is loved, treasured and cared for.

Take the first step today.

Surely you have granted him unending blessings and made
him glad with the joy of Your presence. For the king
trusts in the Lord; through the unfailing love
of the Most High he will not be shaken.
Psalm 21:6-7

November 30

*H*ow can I reach your soul, dear one? I want to reach you in the very deepest part of your being. It pains Me to see that you are resisting a total commitment to Me.

Yes, you enjoy the warm, fuzzy thoughts of My love, but have you totally accepted Me and the life I offer you?

Open the door, beloved, and let the light of My presence into your soul. Let it shine on your face. Stand and bask in the complete fulfillment of total surrender. Let Me fill you with pure undulated joy and peace.

Catch it now, at this time. What you feel here for only a moment is but an essence of what you will feel forever in Heaven. Then it will be complete forever and always.

Catch a glimpse of it, beloved one.

Come to Me now, on bended knee, sitting, or standing tall. Close your eyes and ask for My presence. Give your life to Me and allow Me to forgive your sins by cleansing you in the blood of Jesus. And breathe in My total, complete love.

Let the light bask over you for this moment. This moment today.

Soon it will be forever, My love. Oh, what complete joy!!

For God, Who said, "Let light shine out of darkness," made His
light shine in our hearts to give us the light of the knowledge
of God's glory displayed in the face of Christ.
2 Corinthians 4:6

December 01

*S*ide by side we will walk today. Side by side, step by step into and through the most difficult of situations. I will shine favor upon you. You are My treasure, My love.

There is no situation so difficult that together we cannot walk through it. There is no mountain so high we cannot get to the top and reach the shallow of the other side!

Never fear, beloved one.

You have been facing tough times. Do not be tempted to give up. Never feel that I have left you alone. I am always beside you. Together we will get through this. Take it one day at a time. Each day we will handle it together.

There is joy on the other side of this, beloved one. Such joy. Keep your eyes focused on Me and My love for you. Nothing else is important right now.

Just rest in the absolute knowledge that I know, that I care, and that I am beside you.

You are not alone, My child.
We will get through this together.

You and Me. Me and you.

Consider it pure joy, my brothers and sisters, whenever you face trials of many kinds, because you know that the testing of your faith produces perseverance.
James 1:2-3

December 02

Everlasting love. Something that you cannot experience between each other on earth because of sin.

Everlasting love. A full circle like the rings you wear as a sign of marriage that can last as long as you abide here on earth.

The unbroken circle.

With My everlasting love, I have put a circle around your entire being. From the time I planned you from inside the womb in infancy, through your youth and all your life, I have encircled you with an everlasting band of love. It will never die or even diminish when your days here on earth are over.

I will always hold you within that circle, My love.
Now and forever.

It is not just a circle of love for you, it is a visible circle to those of us in the other world. A mark that you are Mine.

Now and forever. Everlasting love.
Amen

The life of mortals is like grass, they flourish like a flower of the field; the wind blows over it and it is gone, and its place remembers it no more. But from everlasting to everlasting the Lord's love is with those who fear Him.
Psalm 103:15-17

December 03

Each day on earth contains twenty-four hours, twenty-four of which I lovingly planned out for you before you were born.

Not two, not seven, not nineteen, but twenty-four hours.

Surrender your life to Me and let Me show you what I have in store for you every single one of those hours.

Do not twist away from Me and try to do things on your own. Surrender all of your life, all of your schedule, all of your concerns, wholeheartedly to Me.

Come to Me now, beloved child, today and forever, and let Me guide you.

The Lord will guide you always; He will satisfy your needs in
a sun-scorched land and will strengthen your frame.
You will be like a well-watered garden, like
a spring whose waters never fail.
Isaiah 58:11

December 04

I have My eyes on everything you are concerned about. I see you wherever you are, with whatever you are worried about. Your worries are My concerns. I just need you to gently relax into My loving care.

Learning to let go of how you think you are handling things and then giving it up to Me is the hardest thing for you to do. I'm going to say this lovingly, but your attempts to handle things are miniscule compared to what I can do and what I will do, if you let Me.

Does that mean I want you to sit and do nothing? No. Lay the situation at My feet, totally surrendering it. I will guide you from there. You may, in fact, have to work very hard or I might put the right people in front of you who will be able to help you.

Totally surrendering it to Me is your first step. We will work together on It. Not with just your problems but with your relationships, your eating and exercising habits, your jobs, your future. Everything.

You see, I surrendered Jesus for you. Our pain and sacrifice knew no bounds. I gave My love and commitment to you, forming an everlasting covenant between us.

So, come to Me now, wrapped in the knowledge of the covenant of My love, and lay your burdens down at My feet. Oh, the joy you will feel as I flood your soul with peace!

I love you, My child. It's all about trust.

But blessed is the one who trusts in the Lord,
whose confidence is in Him.
Jeremiah 17:7

December 05

My beloved child, wrap yourself in the warmth of My embrace. Let Me fill you with the serene peace only I can give you. You will not find it in the bustle of the world, or even in the embrace of your loved one. It is a gift only I can give you. Rest in it now.

In this day you will have trouble. I will not take you out of the trouble but will be beside you, guiding and directing you, holding your hand, never leaving your side. Together we can face anything. Absolutely anything, and everything. And I know, dear one. I know.

Do not think I am up in some ivory tower unaware of your troubles and your pain. I am beside you, longing to comfort you and take care of you.

But if I am beside you, why are you experiencing the hardships you are? Am I really a caring God who loves you? Why don't I stop the pain? If only I could tell you. But you must trust My love. I see the whole plan. I know what is best not only for this life, but for your eternal life. I know the people around you who are touched by you, by what you say, or what you do, or how, even though you are hurting, you reach out to help them. And how they are helped when they reach out to you.

Trust My love, dear one. There is joy in surrendering your pain at the cross. Give it up to Me. Do not doubt Me. I suffer intense pain when you hurt and turn away from Me because of it. Oh, how I long to hold and comfort you! Lay your pain at the foot of the cross.

Shine with the fullness of My presence in you.

> *"In this world you will have trouble. But take heart!*
> *I have overcome the world."*
> *John 16:33*

December 06

*H*ere I am, My child. Ready again to reassure you of My love for you in every way, every day.

My love and mercy for you extends far past the reaches of your understanding. Never feel that anything stands between us.

How I long to teach you truths from your past, from your own life! Things you might have wondered about but don't have the answers to, or that you have been too reluctant to focus on.

Before now these things were too painful for you to know about or understand. But I feel that soon you will be ready to hear the truth. Soon it will be revealed.

Until that time, lay your head on My chest and let Me tenderly hold you in My arms. In Deuteronomy 33 it is recorded that I said to Moses, "Let My beloved rest secure in Me, for I shield him all day long, and the one I love rests between My shoulders."

I love you, dear one.

Come now, and rest between My shoulders in the shelter of My grace.

> *"Let the beloved of the Lord rest secure in Him, for He*
> *shields him all day long, and the one the Lord*
> *loves rests between His shoulders."*
> *Deuteronomy 33:12*

December 07

*E*ven now in the reaches of your soul, I am stirring memories of Me, of My love and care for you.

Do you remember how you were guided through that situation not long ago? Somehow you knew where to go and what to do.

That was Me.

Were you feeling alone and hurt? I put My arms around you.

Did you feel that there was no way you could continue on any longer, but then, somehow, you were able to gather the strength and get through it?

That was when I picked you up and carried you.

When I see you so concerned, I wish our time on earth was over and I could open your eyes and clearly reveal My absolute presence and complete love in your life. Then you would never feel alone or afraid.

Look for the signs of My gifts to you in the sky: in the glorious sunrise, the beautiful sunsets and the colorful lights playing through cloud formations.

Be reassured, My love, for I am with you always.

"And surely I am with you always, to
the very end of the age."
Matthew 28:20

December 08

As we near the season that you celebrate My Son's birth, do not let your guard down. The enemy is desperate, and approaches on every side, trying to get the focus off Jesus and putting it on all the stress of the holiday season: money for presents, time to buy them and party after party.

Remember the Baby born in a small manger in a rugged barn. He was the Ruler of the universe, come down as human and God, to be raised on earth, visible to man. Visible so He could be better understood and hoped for.

Love poured from His very being. Even without healing miracles, people thronged around Him because of the love. Those with receptive hearts were given the ability to sense it. In total love, He finished His mission on the cross.

Never forget, dear one, when you run into the busyness of this season, the reason behind it: the sacrifice that small Child in a manger made for you and for others.

Never forget. When you pick out your gifts, think of Him. To honor Him, it most likely won't be the largest gift but it will be the most meaningful one, perhaps given of your time or heart rather than your money, but always given with your love: the heart of Love that this season embraces.

Never forget the baby born so far away in such simple circumstances. Never forget His ultimate gift to bring you life with Me forever. That is the message of the season.

For to us a Child is born, to us a Son is given . . . Wonderful
Counselor, Mighty God, Everlasting Father, Prince of Peace.
Isaiah 9:6

December 09

℃ome to Me, My child, and learn of the great things I have done for My people in the past.

Read the stories in the Bible over and over, knowing that one day your eyes will be opened to understand how I am working profoundly in the earth today. Because I don't speak as directly now as I did then, My people often don't know how active I am in world events.

Everything is held in the palm of My hand. Nations, wars, rulers, all the way down to the precious, innocent, child.

Literally everything.

So, every morning when you first stir, bring your thoughts up to Me. Say, "I choose You, Lord, no matter what happens."

If your world seems to fall apart, keep saying "I choose You!" With Me you have love and security, no matter what.

Then arise, and spend time letting Me talk to you through My written Word. Do the best you can with the abilities I have blessed you with to fulfill the mission I have given you, and to reach out and help others.

Then come home and rest in My arms again.

I have the whole world in My hands, dear one, but you are in My arms.

"It is written in the Prophets: 'They will all be taught by
God.' Everyone who has heard the Father and
learned from Him comes to Me."
John 6:45

December 10

See the wind rustling through the trees as it gently blows. I have sent My Holy Spirit to move through you that way with constant messages from Me.

If you stay receptive, you will sense My guidance as I watch over you and work through you in this way.

Stay aware by talking to Me constantly in your thoughts, lest others think you odd!!

These gentle urgings in your soul are the way I will answer your life's greatest questions. Do I keep my job? Do I go forward in this? Is this the person I am supposed to meet?

I am by your side, communicating with you in a very real way. When you dedicated your life to Me, I gave you the gift of the Holy Spirit to work in you, refining and guiding you.

You never need to fear, beloved one.

I will always be beside you, guiding you, directing you and loving you.

Now and forever more.

And you also were included in Christ when you heard the
message of truth, the gospel of your salvation. When you
believed, you were marked in Him with a seal, the promised
Holy Spirit, Who is a deposit guaranteeing our inheritance
until the redemption of those who are God's
possession - to the praise of His glory.
Ephesians 1:13-14

December 11

As the sun rises in the morning, so I reveal My love for you as the unveiling of My majesty.

Let its joy permeate your soul.

When Christ was crucified on the cross, I tore the veil of the temple in two, signifying the end of the old covenant. My new covenant started at the cross. It enables you to come to Me directly with the assurance of My love and care for you.

Think of that as you watch the slowly rising beauty of the daily new dawn. Never failing, the sun rises, sets, and then rises again.

I will never fail you, never change and never give up on you.

Let the light of the new dawn flood your face as you give thanks for the joy of the new covenant I made with you on Calvary, for you are Mine, beloved, bought with a price, a very precious Price.

Let the morning's light shine on your face as you praise My name.

For this reason Christ is the mediator of a new covenant, that those who are called may receive the promised eternal inheritance - now that He has died as a ransom to set them free from the sins committed under the first covenant.
Hebrews 9:15

December 12

Oh, dear child, in the recesses of your soul you have doubts. Like "doubting Thomas", you have so many unanswered questions.

Do you, too, need to see the nail marks in My hands to believe unequivocally that I am a very real Presence in your life?

Dear one, stretch your mind across the sands of time: My time, not yours.

Look up to the Heavens and watch the rolling clouds. Envision things as they were in Christ's time on earth. See how the people loved Him, how they were simply attracted to His presence.

When He spoke, He spoke in a normal tone, yet all around could hear Him. Everyone stopped to listen to Him, and they followed Him wherever He went. They responded to His love, the love that emanated from every fiber of His being.

When they met His gaze, they knew.
His chosen ones knew.

I am here now, feeling your pain, knowing you don't understand My ways. But I am real, beloved, and I will move heaven and earth for you when the time is right: My time, not yours.

Come and take My nail-scarred hand.
Let our joy be complete.

"Put your finger here; see My hands. Reach out your hand
and put it into My side. Stop doubting and believe."
John 20:27

December 13

My beloved child, I yearn for you to know Me, to really know Me. To trust Me. To smile when problems arise, knowing you and I can walk through them together.

If you don't know how to walk through the pain, or if you feel you can't, I will guide you.

I have given you strength you don't realize you have.

The knowledge of Me comes from time spent in My Word, but also in time spent praising Me, lifting your hands to Heaven and calling My name.

Such praise and worship will never go unnoticed.

I will draw closer to you in a more intimate way. My communion with you will be more revealing and you will learn to sense My urgings in a real way.

Come to Me this morning with arms up-raised.

The Savior of the universe is smiling upon you!!

The Lord is my strength and my shield; my heart trusts in Him, and He helps me. My heart leaps for joy, and with my song I praise Him.
Psalm 28:7

December 14

In the shelter of My love comes a peace only you can experience; a peace I share solely with you.

My relationship with you is different than with any other because there is no one like you. I ordained when, where and with whom you would be raised.

No two lives are the same. Each of My children are vastly different.

How does that affect our relationship? I draw near to you in a way only you and I can understand. I fulfill needs only you have, needs only I know you have.

Come to the shelter of the arms of the One Who created you and loves you more than you can ever understand.

There is joy, beauty and peace with Me, beloved one:
the deep contentment only I bestow on only you.

And the peace of God, which transcends all understanding,
will guard your hearts and your minds in Christ Jesus.
Philippians 4:7

December 15

Focus, My child, on what you know, on what I have revealed to you in the past. Focus on those memories these upcoming days.

When you feel frightened or insecure in any way, remember the list of miracles and answered prayer I asked you to write down. Read them over and know I am with you still.

Now and forevermore.

Today will be a special day between us if you make it so. Come to Me in your quiet place so I can commune with you even deeper. Let Me infuse your soul with the knowledge of My love and pleasure in you, My beloved child.

In amidst all your troubles, today will be special, dear one, because you will have My joy dwelling within you . . . My total peace.

There is a bond between us that the evil one and all the problems he brings can never break. Hang on to it today, dear one.

You are in Me and I am in you.

"Righteous Father, though the world does not know you, I know You, and they know that You have sent Me. I have made You known to them, and will continue to make You known in order that the love You have for Me may be in them and that I Myself may be in them."
John 17:25-26

December 16

The Christmas season is upon you now, one of love and goodwill. This time is especially hard for many people because of the acute loneliness they feel. In all your busyness, do not forget to reach out to them.

You may not realize who they are, but there are many broken souls all around you. Listen to My gentle urgings. Don't let someone pass you by who I point out to you. Reach over and give them a hug, give them something to eat, or invite them over. Do something that makes them feel they are not alone in this world.

You have the incredible gift of My love that I reveal to you. Share it with them. You are My lifeline to others.

Help them to learn, beloved one. You are My chosen one not only to love and take to Heaven to live with Me forever, but I have chosen you to spread the news of My love and salvation to the world. Much of the world doesn't know Me, dear one.

No fancy words are needed. Just share who I am to you. I will do the rest, with every step, every word. My precious soldier-in-training just got booted up!

Reach out and touch someone with the gift I have given you. The Gift of the love of My Son, which is celebrated this season.

Make the season real.

As it is written:
"How beautiful are the feet of those who bring good news!"
Romans 10:15

December 17

At the onset of the day, write your tasks down, all the things you wish to get done in the daylight hours. Then, during your prayer time, turn the list over to Me, asking for My help and guidance.

Together we will go through the day, accomplishing as much as I know you should do.

By committing your day to Me, you are honoring Me with your time and devotion. I will honor that, My cherished one, and help you with wisdom and power.

See how wonderful and easy it is to be connected to such a Father? I can't say it will always be easy, as I will ask you to walk at times where you do not choose to walk, but I am ever with you, watching even your tiniest steps.

Commit your way to Me, beloved one, at the opening of the day.

Remember how I have led you in the past and know that I will never let you go.

Commit your way to the Lord; trust in Him and He will do this: He will make your righteous reward shine like the dawn, your vindication like the noonday sun.
Psalm 37:5-6

December 18

How can I forget you, dear one? You are the apple of My eye, one of My precious joys. I hear every word you utter, every precious prayer you send to Me. Each one of them is held in the palm of My hand and is answered, either right away, or when the time is right.

Your prayers rise up to Me like sacred vessels. They are covered with your tears, your joy, or just your everyday concerns about your life or for others'. They arrive in the Holy Place where they are recorded and answered.

Every word you send to Me in Jesus' name is answered. You are My love and My joy. Our line of communication is clear and strong when you stay connected to Me.

Do not stray, beloved. There is so much at stake. Call out to Me in Jesus' name. There is real power there.

Remember I hear your every word and your every thought. You are talking directly to Me, as if you were at My feet.

Come to Me now with your requests and praise. Let Me cover you with My love and grace.

You will know the answers, beloved one.
When the time is right, you will know.

The prayer of a righteous person
is powerful and effective.
James 5:16

December 19

*E*very drop of rain that falls on your head I know. I see you standing out in a busy crowd when you think you are alone and unnoticed.

So noticeable you are, dear one!

To the Father Who loves you so much, you stand out in any crowd! You are like a dove alighting on a magnificent elm tree, so beautiful and with such grace.

You are My dove to the world.

Because of your relationship with Me, I send you out to reach others to help them. Most of the time, you don't even realize it. You carry Me inside of you, and through you I am able to reach out to touch others.

Every single thing you do every day is important to Me.
You are important to Me.

Shine where you are. In your greatest pain, reach out to bring joy to someone else. How heaven rejoices! Tears of joy are shed by the heavenly host watching good play out against evil.

You are never lost in a crowd, dear one.
My love for you is so great I know where you are at any moment.

For you are Mine, beloved, and I am yours.

Your ways, God, are holy. What god is as great as our God?
You are the God Who performs miracles; You display
Your power among the peoples.
Psalm 77:13-14

December 20

$\mathcal{L}$ook around the home you live in. Is it large or small? Do you have simple things or nice things? Do you know I could live anywhere with you? That the King of the Universe would dwell anywhere that His beloved child is?

Don't run around spending all your time and money fixing up your home, or buying the latest, most expensive clothes or cars. I provided you with the money and opportunity you have.

I love you just as you are.

First, give back to Me. That is all I ask. No matter what you receive, give a portion of it back in service to Me. And remember, I will bless you.

One day we will live together forever, no matter where you live now or what your circumstances are.

I don't need a big mansion, My child. I only need your love.

Come, take My hand. Let the joy begin.

"Bring the whole tithe into the storehouse, that there may be
food in My house. Test me in this," says the Lord Almighty,
"and see if I will not throw open the floodgates of heaven
and pour out so much blessing that there will not
be room enough to store it.
Malachi 3:10

December 21

For all your troubles today, think of Me. Through the vast array of things that pop up in front of you to be handled, think of Me.

Keep Me ever in your heart and mind so that you will never be without courage or wisdom. I promise you both through these challenging times. You never need to fear any crisis that arises because I have given you the tools to successfully deal with them.

Does that mean I will always grant you success? No. I will always grant you courage and wisdom to face anything head on, knowing that all things will work out for the best because you have chosen to love and serve Me.

All of My children are different. Some drive big cars, some drive simple ones. Some live in large houses, and others live in small rental units. Each were created by Me and for Me, to fulfill My purpose here on earth.

Tap into that courage and wisdom, dear one, so that no matter what faces you here, you may know My complete joy.

The fear of the Lord is the beginning of wisdom; all who
follow His precepts have good understanding.
To Him belongs eternal praise.
Psalm 111:10

December 22

Are you ready? Are you ready for what I have planned for you?

Stop looking at your limitations, worrying about your daily life. Put it in My hands and I will carry the load for you because I have other things I want you to think about.

I want you to look up to Me, spread your arms out wide and breathe Me in. Surrender yourself to Me in this way, honoring and praising Me. I will infuse your soul anew with the Holy Spirit Who lives in you to guide and direct you.

The plans I have for you are so much bigger than what you had imagined. I have only begun to work in you and through you.

If you could see the end from the beginning you would be so amazed!

You are Mine.

I CHOSE YOU to be on the forefront of My work here on earth. People are watching you because they see Me in you. No matter where you are, in simple circumstances or in grand towers, I have a mighty purpose for you.

Be ready, beloved one.
Right here. Right now.

Instead, speaking the truth in love, we will grow to become in every respect the mature body of Him who is the head, that is, Christ. From Him the whole body, joined and held together by every supporting ligament, grows and builds itself up in love, as each part does its work.
Ephesians 4:15-16

December 23

Today is a new day! Rejoice, dear child of Mine, for you have been chosen to deliver My message of love and righteousness to others.

Me, you ask? Yes, you.

With Me at your side, you are a mighty warrior and I will provide you with words and timing.

I'm not talking about standing on the street corners. I have others to do that. I am talking about touching the lives of those you come in contact with on a daily basis. Not preaching to them about hell and damnation, but gently sharing the story of My love: the Gospel of Jesus Christ Who came to earth as a baby boy, and His life and death for them, His resurrection that gives hope to all mankind who will accept it's truth into their lives.

You can share this truth, loved one, because it has grown real in your life. I have grown real in your life. Let others know that they, too, may have an intimate walk with Me.

I will give you just the right words at the right time.

Stay close, dear one.
Our journey has just begun!

> *Although I am less than the least of all the Lord's people, this grace was given me: to preach to the Gentiles the boundless riches of Christ, and to make plain to everyone the administration of this mystery, which for ages past was kept hidden in God, Who created all things.*
> *Ephesians 3:8-9*

December 24

When you are in the right frame of mind, when you are in your quiet place and I am able to talk more directly with you, I will unfold the most marvelous truths to you: the truths of how near and dear you are to Me, how I have always loved you, how I have never abandoned you, and how I am always by your side.

Sometimes you envision our relationship like the father figure you know on earth. If it was good, you have no problems coming to Me. But if it was bad, you have a hard time letting go of the anger or pain, even fear, and sometimes, it is your imagination of who I am.

How that hurts Me, beloved one!
Do not mistake the love I have for you, the sacrifice of My Son's death on the cross, for you, to equal the love you might have received here on earth.

I will never leave you, I will never let you down.
I gave the ultimate sacrifice of love for you.

No matter what has happened on earth, come to me anew every morning and let Me unfold the story of My marvelous love to you. Let My joy fill every part of your body, from your head to the tips of your toes.

You can have that joy, My child. Just come to Me. Open your Bible or just close your eyes and pray. I will come and surround you.

You are Mine and I am yours.

You make known to me the path of life; You will fill me
with joy in Your presence, with eternal
pleasures at Your right hand.
Psalm 16:11

December 25

Today is the day you celebrate the birth of the precious Savior of the world Who eschewed the grandeur and power of Heaven to come to earth as a vulnerable, poor child. I watched that magical night as Mary and Joseph counted His fingers and toes in wonder at His perfection.

Only I totally understood Jesus' purpose. Only I knew how His 33 years on earth would be played out. Only I understood the tremendous sorrow and pain as He took the world's sin upon His shoulders and I separated Myself from Him, allowing Him to die to become the Victor for all mankind.

As you unwrap and share gifts with others, remember the reason for the giving and loving. Think of that beautiful scene in the barn, the beginning of the sacrifice that was made so that We could be with you.

Take it personally, my child, for it was for you that He came. It was for you that He died. It was for you that He rose again from the dead.

With joy and love, rise up and take your place among My chosen ones. Let Heaven's light shine upon you as you honor His birth today.

Exalt the Love that has no match.
IT IS LOVE DEFINED.

> *I bring you good news that will cause great joy for all the people. Today in the town of David a Savior has been born to you; He is the Messiah, the Lord . . . Glory to God in the highest heaven, and on earth peace to those on whom His favor rests.*
> *Luke 2:10-11,14*

December 26

*H*ow the morning speaks of My love!

When all the earth is washed anew with freshness and new beginnings, so is My hope for you each day. Then you will come before Me to renew your dedication and when you do, I will open a whole new world to you each and every day.

Start it with fresh anticipation of the wonders of My love, eagerly facing the challenges that are put in front of you, knowing I am beside you.

At the end of the day, come back to Me and to your quiet place to reflect on what we have accomplished.

There is much only I can see.

Your life was not the only one enriched by our connection. It has made a difference in others' lives as well.

Truly you walk, truly you will see and one day, and truly you will know.

And hope does not put us to shame, because God's love
has been poured out into our hearts through the
Holy Spirit, Who has been given to us.
Romans 5:5

December 27

℘ome and sing a new song to Me, a song of your everlasting love and devotion. Fill the corners of the heavens with your praise so that the angelic hosts may rejoice with you.

Rejoice in your salvation. Rejoice in your life. Rejoice in the family I have given you. Rejoice in the family of friends that surround you.

Rejoice, I say, rejoice!
What sweetness fills My soul at this!

I will draw ever nearer to you as you learn to praise My Name more and more.

Everywhere you walk in praise, creation rejoices. Birds sing, frogs leap, swans glide, fish team. All have their ways to praise Me and when one of My own starts the chorus, they all join in the joy.

Let it be well with your soul, dear one. Let all the cares of earth slip from your shoulders as you join all creation praising My name.

I will fill you with a peace that passes all understanding. Dwell with Me on the mountain of hope and salvation, far away from the pit of darkness of the world and it's cares.

You and I are one, dear one.
That's all that matters.

All people will fear; they will proclaim the works of God and
ponder what He has done. The righteous will rejoice in
the Lord and take refuge in Him; all the upright
in heart will glory in Him!
Psalm 64:9-10

December 28

As the sirens race around in the darkness, and you wonder what trouble is behind the noise, focus your mind on Me.

Do not be disturbed by what you feel is reality here. This will not be a meaningless, scary world for you when you keep your focus on Me.

Behind the signs of the end times stands a heavenly Father Who loves you more than you can imagine, and Who will guide you through everything.

I am not asking you to ignore these signs, but to take hope in them, knowing your time here is nearing an end. Although frightened by the thought, you should be filled with anticipation of our time together being complete.

We are close, dear one. Stay focused on Me.

When bad things happen, know that I am stronger than it all, I have overcome the world, and that I love you and will always take care of you.

So do not fear the sirens or the future. Everything that happens has been in place since the foundation of the world.

And you, dear one, were in My mind then.

Lift up your eyes to the heavens, look at the earth beneath; the heavens will vanish like smoke, the earth will wear out like a garment and its inhabitants die like flies. But My salvation will last forever, My righteousness will never fail.
Isaiah 51:6

December 29

*H*ow I long to hold you in My arms and cast out all your fears! A little while longer, beloved one, and all will be well.

I am your Rock; lean on Me. I am your Foundation, the Answer to your questions, from beginning to end.

Come and lay your head against My chest and dream with Me. Dream of a new land, one with golden days, blue skies, tall mountains, grassy plains.

A land where there is no more pain and suffering, where the mighty lion will lay down with the gentle lamb.

You are My lamb, dear one.

I hold you close in My heart and mind always. When the time is right, I will gather you unto Myself and we will roam together in absolute joy.

The days are very troubled on earth, and the end of time is coming soon.

Hold on tightly and never let go, for I am your Rock and your Foundation through all of life's storm.

Soon, dear one. Soon.

> *The Lord is exalted, for He dwells on high; He will fill Zion*
> *with His justice and righteousness. He will be the sure*
> *foundation for your times, a rich store of salvation*
> *and wisdom and knowledge; the fear of the*
> *Lord is the key to this treasure.*
> *Isaiah 33:5-6*

December 30

Every day is a new beginning, a fresh start with Me and the world. A time to learn and a time to grow.

What would I like you to learn?

Today will be full of life-teaching moments. If you were not walking with Me, you would not see or understand them.

At the end of the day, think back and see what was a life lesson. Was it from an error you made, was it something the Holy Spirit directed you to, or did you have an earthly teacher?

Every day I put in front of you lessons I want you to learn from. Each day is an important step towards eternal life with Me. Learn to treasure each and every one. Make each day a valuable and precious time to grow into a closer relationship with Me.

And listen. Listen to the gentle urgings of My Holy Spirit.

He is near. He is here.

He is My Word in you. He is the love I fill you with.

Listen, dear one. Listen and learn.

Show me Your ways, Lord, teach me Your paths. Guide me in
Your truth and teach me, for You are God my Savior,
and my hope is in You all day long.
Psalm 25:4-5

December 31

Today you have many thoughts of new beginnings as the year dawns.

Use this time of earthly celebration to write down the positive changes I have encouraged you to make. Don't let it be all about how you are going to improve yourself. Honoring your body as My temple is important, but also have it be about how you are going to help others I have placed around you.

And most importantly, let it be about the steps you are going to take to draw nearer to Me. Without this step, the first two will not be fully possible.

Let the mark of this new year be a new beginning for us. Come and walk closer and closer to Me. Commit time each morning when you will pray and rededicate your life to Me.

My heart is filled to overflowing when you come to Me in a broken and contrite spirit and I am able to fill your life with My love and surround you with My protective armor throughout the day. If you make this first day the start of daily committing yourself totally to Me, everything else will fall into place.

How proud I am of you, dear one.

Don't look back or be discouraged by the past. Face the future with hope and joy, and the peace of knowing you are in the arms of a loving Savior Who will guide your every step.

*"So may all your enemies perish, Lord! But may all who love
You be like the sun when it rises in its strength."*
Judges 5:31